South Florida's Fishing Paradise

Early Adventures Fishing from Alligator Alley to Boca Grande

James Stenson

STACKPOLE BOOKS

Essex, Connecticut
Blue Ridge Summit, Pennsylvania

STACKPOLE BOOKS

An imprint of Globe Pequot, the trade division of The Rowman & Littlefield Publishing Group, Inc.
4501 Forbes Blvd., Ste. 200
Lanham, MD 20706
www.rowman.com

Distributed by NATIONAL BOOK NETWORK

British Library Cataloguing in Publication Information Available

Library of Congress Cataloging-in-Publication Data

Names: Stenson, James, 1957– author.
Title: South Florida's fishing paradise : early adventures from Lake Worth to Florida Bay to Boca Grande and back / James Stenson.
Description: Lanham, MD : Stackpole Books, an imprint of Globe Pequot, the trade division of The Rowman & Littlefield Publishing Group, Inc., [2023] | Summary: "Jim Stenson chronicles his fishing adventures from Sanibel to the tarpon capital of the world-Boca Grande-to rivers like the Manatee and the Myakka. In addition to being an immensely entertaining read with a colorful cast of characters, the book has a strong environmental message"—Provided by publisher.
Identifiers: LCCN 2022041073 (print) | LCCN 2022041074 (ebook) | ISBN 9780811772525 (paperback) | ISBN 9780811772556 (epub)
Subjects: LCSH: Fishing—Florida—Boca Grande. | Fishing—Florida—Everglades Parkway.
Classification: LCC SH441 .S815 2023 (print) | LCC SH441 (ebook) | DDC 799.109759/39—dc23/eng/20221118
LC record available at https://lccn.loc.gov/2022041073
LC ebook record available at https://lccn.loc.gov/2022041074

For my wife, Sandra, who put up with the aggravation and the endless hours listening to me complain about anything and everything that has to do with publishing a book. That said, I love you exponentially more than you love me! I couldn't have done it without you.

Contents

Acknowledgments

*W*riting is hard work, and, like fly-fishing, it takes time and hard-won experience to write well. You have to have the time to write, which is usually the first obstacle. Then you have to love to write. Unfortunately, that love seems to ebb and flood like the tide. And then you have to develop the skills to write. Even more crucial, you have to have the stories to begin with.

Nothing in life happens in a vacuum: to be successful, you need the support of your family and friends. In my case, it was my wife, Sandra, and my closest friend, Walter Winton. Every morning during the pandemic, Walt and I spent hours on the phone rereading and editing *South Florida's Fishing Paradise*. We both grew up in Fort Lauderdale. Even though we didn't know each other, we shared the same stories, the same piers, and the same fish. He was the perfect candidate. Walt understood the local jargon. Without the back-and-forth daily banter with Walt and the motivation of my wife, *South Florida's Fishing Paradise* probably never would have seen the light of day.

I would also like to thank Norm Ziegler and Alan Kennedy for their support—and for taking the time to spend long hours on the phone discussing books, writers, and all things fly-fishing (especially the days we sat around Norm's fly shop on Sanibel, downing fried grouper sandwiches and french fries from The Island Cow).

Introduction

When I set out to write this book I immediately sensed a danger looming. It was that I was almost bound to fall into the trap of nostalgia and indignation, of turning this book into a diatribe against the passing of the original Florida. Because to anyone who has known Florida as long as I have, and whose interest in the place has been its wild landscapes and wild creatures, the losses have been the most spectacular events of the past three decades.

—Archie Carr, *A Naturalist in Florida*

*A*ll great rivers run to the ocean and, at the confluence where the sweet meets the brine, there's an explosion of life that has few equals. It's a place where the majority of the sport's greatest game fish congregate and, in essence, it's the cradle of some of the best saltwater fly-fishing on the planet. I was lucky enough to grow up in a place just like that—South Florida and the Florida Keys. I didn't realize it at the time, but for a kid who loved to fish, it was paradise.

While other kids were fishing farm ponds for pan fish and bass or small streams for brook trout, I was pitching flies at snook and tarpon, and when I had the chance, bonefish and permit. I grew up in what most old-timers considered the glory days of the Miami Metropolitan Fishing Tournament. The MET was a legendary fishing competition in Miami that ran between mid-December and mid-April. In the early days, it was primarily a guide's tournament. But by the time I came along, it had opened to anyone who had the time and money—and, yes, more often than not, money and free time dictated the winners.

My fishing buddies and I grew up in South Florida fishing estuaries with colorful names such as Biscayne Bay, Florida Bay, Charlotte Harbor, the Indian River Lagoon, the Florida Keys of course, and maybe the mother of all estuaries—the Ten Thousand Islands. We fished the Myakka River, the Peace River, the Caloosahatchee, the Indian and Banana Rivers, and the undulating "river of grass"—the Florida Everglades. When we were old enough to sponge a ride off someone who had a valid driver's license and, better yet, access to his parents' car, we ventured north—beyond the range of our trusty bicycles. One's home water is normally defined by and predicated on transportation—or the lack thereof. We fished the Kissimmee Basin down through the random canals and potholes that make up the northern reaches of Lake Okeechobee.

My formative years were spent in Fort Lauderdale, appropriately nick-named Fort Liquordale—a city that's better known for its rowdy spring break and the multitudes of strip clubs that line US 1 than for its fishing. The appellation Fort Liquordale was given to the town because of the voluminous amount of rum smuggled in from the Caribbean during Prohibition, and the vast number of mob-run speakeasies that operated unchecked by the feds and the local authorities in the early days of that failed social experiment.

Back then, Florida ranked as the ninth most populous state—just shy of seven million people. But, of course, every winter the snowbirds showed up, and the population doubled. Fast-forward forty years, the population is approaching twenty-five million and growing every year at a seemingly uncontrollable rate. One can only ponder what the population is in the wintertime when the multitudes of domestic and international tourists migrate south. I know this might be hard for those familiar with the region to believe, but when I was a fledgling youth; there were green spaces between Fort Lauderdale and Miami, and Pompano and Palm Beach to the north. The west coast south of Tampa was dotted with small towns that were nothing more than citrus groves. Naples, now one of the nation's most affluent cities with the sixth highest income per capita, was a sleepy fishing village known as the little town at the other end of the Tamiami Canal.

Off the west coast of Florida lie the barrier islands; comprised of almost pure milky quartz of recent geologic origin, they count among the whitest sand beaches in the world. The pristine white sands originated in the Piedmont, a plateau region in the eastern United States, washed to the gulf by rivers, and refined through the timeless reworking of wind and waves into sand of uniform size. The geological result was simply magical and, regret-tably, irresistible to land developers. Back in those innocent days of my youth, the barrier islands that run along the west coast had not yet been developed, or at least were only partially developed, compared to the ruination that now constitutes southwest Florida. Charlotte Harbor was considered one of the last great nurseries left on the west coast. The harbor itself was pristine, and the fishing was, well, in a word, indescribable. The mangroves had not yet been cut down for the tasteless condos that now line the harbor like a picket fence made of concrete blocks and sheetrock, each a testimony to just how bland architecture has become in this country.

I remember a harbor knee-deep in turtle grass and home to some of the most prolific clam beds on the west coast, where the river and creek mouths were smothered in thick layers of oyster beds. It was idyllic. The bird population had few equals and, because Charlotte Harbor lies directly in the path of the eastern flyway, the spring and fall migrations resulted in an astonishing number of bird species. From an angler's perspective, it was, hands down, the best fly-fishing on the west coast.

The waters ran clear, except where the Myakka, the Peace, and the Caloosahatchee Rivers dumped their nutrient-rich waters into the briny waters of Charlotte Harbor. That serendipitous balance of sweet water and brine created one of the most bountiful aquatic nurseries in the state of Florida, maybe the world: it was Biscayne Bay on steroids. The quantity of biomass staggered the mind. The flora and fauna were unparalleled in the southeastern United States. Better yet, and maybe more to the point, it was right in my backyard. Of course, in those days, I considered the whole of South Florida my personal backyard.

South Florida is home to more saltwater and freshwater canals than you could fish in a lifetime, and a good many of them are brackish. If the water is not too briny, you can catch both freshwater and saltwater fish in the majority of the canals. Even if the water is too briny, you'll still find tarpon and snook. At one time in the not-too-distant past, schools of giant jack crevalles proliferated in the canals of South Florida devouring everything in sight.

The crème de la crème of the canal system is the spillway, where a saltwater canal butts up against a freshwater canal with a dam separating the two. Normally, freshwater canals are built at higher elevations, and when the summer rains come (and they always do in South Florida), the water flows over the dams—the more water, the better. Even though South Florida is relatively flat, water flows west to the Gulf of Mexico and east to the Atlantic. Mostly though, it flows south through the Everglades—hence the name "river of grass."

Surprisingly, not all rivers run directly to the ocean. In fact, few rivers do. Most dump into immense harbors and bays, create estuaries, and eventually reach the ocean through passes. A great example is Charlotte Harbor. The Myakka, the Peace, and the Caloosahatchee all run into Charlotte Harbor, and the harbor is full of smaller bays and creeks consistently swept clean by incoming and outgoing tides. Large passes such as Boca Grande and a few smaller ones to the south flush out the harbor twice a day. The volume of water that comes in and out of these passes on any given day is remarkable. In the south, the big river systems move very slowly, and unless it happens to be the rainy season, extremely so.

I have spent my life in these areas chasing some of the world's greatest game fish. Essentially, the world's great estuaries can be divided into two categories: first, cold-water fisheries that evolved in and around the rivers and bays of the North Atlantic and the North Pacific; and second, the estuaries found in the Southern Hemisphere that are located in and around the tropical equatorial regions. These areas are under siege from development, pollution, mining, deforestation, overfishing, and overpopulation. I can't think of one game species that is not a mere shadow of its former glory.

That is what this book is about—not necessarily the fish, but the land itself, the flora and the fauna, the people and the culture that grew up around the estuaries.

It's about the great biodiversity that evolved in these estuaries and, sadly, it's about the loss of that biodiversity. It's about the loss of cultural diversity, too. It's about the native peoples who were either pushed out because of dwindling resources or, in most cases, who couldn't afford to live, or make a living, where they were born. And, of course, it's about the loss of the great game fish that once thrived in some of the most fertile estuaries in the world that have either disappeared or are on the verge of disappearing.

In all, it's about the world in which I grew up, the world I loved.

I once considered myself too headstrong and set in my ways to write something that might be useful, or at least a little entertaining, for others who share my passion for adventure or hard-core travel and fly-fishing. The other consideration has always been the lack of precious time, time to sit in front of a computer and ponder the truly important questions—such as what are the best tides to fish for bonefish during the spring at Deep Water Cay? Then take the time that's necessary to hunker down and write, when the truth is, fly-fishermen would rather be staked out on a briny flat somewhere rather than sitting at a desk pounding away on a keyboard.

Writing is hard work and, like fly-fishing, it takes time and hard-won experience to write well. That being said, I was the managing editor and publisher of *The Contemporary Sportsman* and *The Contemporary Wingshooter* for seven years. Recently, unable to keep my fingers out of the publishing game, I launched the *Sweet Waters Adventure Travel Log*. Because necessity has dictated it, I have learned a little patience and, some might say, even gained a little skill, although my columns and stories were always the last ones in. On more than one occasion, I have been known to hold up the press. I should have written this book many years ago, but like most fishermen I, too, have a difficult time getting off the water, and that has left little time to ruminate or write books. Now, age and environmental exigencies seem to require that I procrastinate no longer.

Finally, a word of caution: don't get in your car or jump on the next airplane and expect to relive what I experienced when I was young. The places still exist, of course, and the fishing to some extent is still viable, but, for the most part, this book is a glimpse of what was and probably never will be again. This book has become a way for me to remember the way it was when I was a young man growing up in the birthplace of the best light tackle saltwater fishing on the planet. Time has given me the perspective to see the changes and the opportunity to reflect and come to terms with the changes that have destroyed one of the things I love most in this world.

As Ed Abbey once wrote, "What I write about in this book is already gone or going under fast. This is a not a travel guide but an elegy. A memorial. You are holding a tombstone in your hands. A bloody rock. Don't drop it on your foot—throw it at something big and glassy. What do you have to lose?"

· 1 ·

Perspective

In my misspent youth, I was part of a group of twenty-five or thirty kids of various ages who grew up on Anglin's Pier where Commercial Boulevard T-bones Lauderdale by the Sea. We were a tribe, a bunch of ragtag kids without a pot to piss in, with little or no parental control. Some grew up fishing, some surfed; others, like myself, did both. Of course, we fished, but when the winter swells rolled in from the northeast, we surfed the morning glass—then chased fish on the incoming tides in the afternoon.

Honestly, the surfing off Fort Lauderdale wasn't exactly Waimea Bay. Not until junior high school did I discover that size and quantity of the waves didn't much matter because it was much easier to meet girls walking down the beach with a surfboard tucked under your arm than it was to meet girls carrying an armload of fishing rods down the pier. Surfers were cool, and in 1969 almost everybody listened to the Beach Boys.

The locals called us pier rats because we were always there, day or night, running up and down the pier in shorts or swim trunks. When the temperatures occasionally dropped into the low sixties in the winter, we slipped into old worn-out T-shirts. You know the ones I'm talking about—the ones your mother always wanted to trash but rarely had the heart to do so, much less tell you about it if she did. We lived in blown-out flip-flops held together by duct tape and faded Miami Dolphins baseball hats. We thrived on cheeseburgers and hot dogs, plus the occasional milkshake.

We rarely had the money to get on the pier, much less afford a good meal at the little mom-and-pop diner at the beginning of the pier. But eventually, we figured out that if we kept the live wells in the tackle shop filled with pilchards and goggle eyes and the freezer filled with mullet and shrimp, there would always be food waiting for us in the diner. I know it probably sounds like child

1

labor, but it was a labor of love. It was a life spent outdoors in the warm sun, the wind, and the waves. Looking back, we were living the dream—a life most kids could only fantasize about.

We chased pilchards and goggle eyes with tiny white quills and small gold hooks under the lights at night using ultralight tackle, so light that today it might look more like a toy. In the spring and fall, we dredged the incoming waves for sand fleas up and down the beaches and sold them to the pompano fishermen for bait. Often in summer, the storms would come thundering out of the southwest, and on the outgoing tides, Biscayne Bay would dump all her riches into the Atlantic. The winds would blow the waves north, and we would line up on the south side of the pier with long dip nets and fill five-gallon buckets with shrimp as they drifted by under the lights. Fresh shrimp were worth their weight in gold—the tourists would pay a small fortune for them.

The tourists also lined the pier dipping shrimp and never noticed all the giant shadows lying underneath the clouds of shrimp. The shadows belonged to massive snook gorging on the shrimp. I mean thirty pounds and up, on many occasions, fish that were just too big to land on the pier. The rub was that to fool one, you had to use an extremely light line and full flex rod with a very light tip. You needed to cast the shrimp out past the shadow line made from the pier lights without any weights and free line the shrimp down current to make it look like a natural shrimp. The lighter the line, the better your chances. You might land two or three snook and lose just as many on a good night. Trying to stop a snook upwards of twenty pounds heading north was too much to ask of a twenty-pound outfit.

South Florida has four distinct seasons. Very few people live in South Florida full-time, and when they visit, they don't seem to stay long enough to appreciate the subtle changes in the seasons. The few who live there full-time rarely venture out of their air-conditioned homes or condos; if they do, it's to shop at the local mall or eat at their favorite restaurants. In fact, it is the change in the seasons that drives the fishing.

Most of the game fish living in the Gulf Stream are pelagic—they move up and down the coast following the baitfish that migrate north in the spring and south in the fall. There is also what I call the "in and out migration" from the sweet to the brine—or primarily from the fresh to the salt. To make life a little more complicated, the migration patterns are very different on the east coast from the west coast. All fish have a tolerance for water temperatures hot and cold, and rarely do they leave their comfort zone.

It's easy, right? You figure out the time of year, the water temperatures, find the bait—and you're in. At one time, it was that easy because there were so many fish and enormous schools of bait that covered what seemed like miles of surface water. The crème de la crème was the spring and fall mullet run. The migration lasted for what seemed like months. You could follow them up and down the east and west coasts—although the runs on the east coast were always more abundant, and the beach fishing was more intense. The tides on the east coast have always been stronger, and the surf is much heavier. At times it was almost dangerous: all you needed to do was skip school, find someone with reasonably good transportation, pitch in a few bucks for gas, and you were on your way. Skipping school in those days was easy; it was the few bucks for gas that presented the problem.

The schools of mullet stretched for nigh on miles; huge tarpon circled and boiled on the surface as if they were playing with the mullet. Giant snook devoured the mullet in the surf and, right when you thought a twenty-five or thirty-pound snook was going to crush your bait, a huge jack crevalle came crashing in and sucked it down. It took everything you could do to hang on to your tarpon rod and not get dragged into the water.

The surf was challenging; the sand, shifty at best. The outgoing current would wash the sand out from under your feet and, if you weren't careful, you with it. Most of this action happened within ten, maybe fifteen feet from the beach. You haven't lived until you've tried to land a pissed-off jack crevalle in raging surf and then had to take the hook out and release him. More often than not, you ended up in the water on your ass with the fish on top of you. It's like paddling out in heavy surf and getting pounded into the sand face first. When you finally make it to the surface, you look around and find out you are only ten feet from the beach.

Sharks of all kinds followed the mullet runs: hammerheads, bull sharks, monster tiger sharks, browns, and enormous amounts of black tips and spinner sharks. Of course, I think the big hammers and bulls were there because they knew the tarpon would be there. After all, why waste your time and energy on a two-pound mullet when you could run down and essentially swallow a hundred-pound tarpon. I know it sounds brutal, but a tarpon is nothing more than an overgrown prehistoric seagoing pilchard to a big hammerhead shark. It strains the imagination until you see a thousand-pound hammerhead up close. It's also hard to fathom just how fast a big predator can move—not to mention that it can turn on a dime. It's a dance that has been going on since long before humans walked on this planet. Everything in the ocean is built on the predator–prey relationship. It's not something you want to get in the middle of. It's both an educational and frightening experience at the same time. It gives new meaning to the expression adrenalin rush.

A few years after the époque of these pages, a couple of close friends and I got the brilliant idea to don a pair of fins and a mask and snorkel, then ease our way into the water to get a better look at what was going on below the surface. I have no idea why—maybe I had been watching too many Jacques Cousteau specials. Most of our friends thought we were just a little off our rockers and pretty much deserved what we got. Looking back, it's not the dumbest idea I have ever had, but it's right up there in the top ten. After all, most of us loved to surf, and we were well accustomed to being underwater, rarely on purpose, but underwater nonetheless. It happened enough times that we considered ourselves accustomed to being slammed into the bottom with some regularity and getting raked over the reef and dumped onto the beach.

As we eased into the water I couldn't help but think this was really a stupid idea. Every time I closed the distance between the mullet and me, the school of mullet moved off. The few game fish we saw pushed into the deeper water. I remember seeing my first shark underwater that day. I had seen plenty of sharks around Anglin's Pier, and, over time, I wouldn't say I had grown unafraid of them, but I wasn't necessarily terrified either. For the most part, surfers spend a tremendous amount of time in the water trying (without success) to ignore the fact we might come face-to-face with a shark one day. When I saw the bull shark underwater, I did my best not to freak out. Still, all I wanted to do was to get the hell out of the water and not get my ass chewed. Like most predators, if there is a tremendous amount of food around, sharks can be rather docile. I learned that from one of Jacques Cousteau's specials. It was something you had to take at face value. After all, Jacques Cousteau wouldn't lie about something so important, would he?

From late fall through early spring, we would stand shoulder to shoulder casting crocks and hooking and landing Spanish mackerel on almost every cast. It was a bloodbath at times. Most of the mackerel ended up on the menus of the local restaurants that lined A1A at the time. To make things a little more hectic, pompano was either mixed in with mackerel, or they soon followed by the thousands. We would pool our resources and fill the coolers with pompano, then knock on the kitchen doors of all the same restaurants that had bought the Spanish mackerel and offer up the pompano to the chef. At the time pompano were so popular with the tourists, we sold every one we could catch.

Spring rolled through like a late summer hurricane in all its petulant moods. It was gone before you knew what hit you. You knew it wouldn't be long before the hectic pace of spring would slow down, and the long, hot, gnarly days of summer would start to take their toll. Everything would change. The tourists always beat feet somewhere around Easter. The weather turned blazing hot; the beaches emptied. Then, the surf (and surfing) died. It would be late September, early October, before we started to see any tropical disturbances that might generate a decent break to surf.

Everything in Nature Is Connected

$\mathcal{D}$uring the long, lazy days of summer, we basically had the pier to our-selves. The heat thinned out the crowds. Even the types of baitfish changed: it was primarily a mix of pilchards and other white baits, although there were always dork jacks under the lights at night, and for the most part, there were still plenty of ballyhoo and goggle eyes in the shadows. As the water warmed up, snook and tarpon showed up in large numbers—numbers you could never imagine today. They were always around just at line's end. But even the pace of fishing slowed down. Compared to spring and fall, it could get downright boring at times.

The one constant was the afternoon thunderstorms. Every afternoon about two-thirty or three o'clock, massive thunderheads came rolling in from the west over Marjory Stoneman Douglas's "river of grass," the Florida Everglades. The massive clouds looked more like giant balls of cotton awash in ivory, blacks, deep ultramarine purples, intense pinks, and washed-out grays billowing up into the atmosphere like a hydrogen bomb that just went off. The thunder could be deafening; the lightning was downright terrifying.

But, over the years, I began to enjoy the storms. Regardless of how old I get, I will always associate summers in south Florida with massive thunder-storms rolling across Marjory's beloved Everglades. It was a slow time, a time to be kids, and from what I remember, it was good to be a kid.

There were times I would show up at the pier, roll out fifteen or twenty rods, and not string up a rod for days. We would stand around and stare into the abyss, just watching and waiting. Waiting for what, who knows? We were always learning from the older kids and trying to imitate every-thing that made them successful. We told stories, and we ragged on each other until we couldn't stop laughing. We spent hours on end in the diner drinking milkshakes, gorging on salty french fries, just talking about the things we loved. For the most part, the conversations always came back to fishing or our beloved Miami Dolphins.

You had to be there to catch fish. There were times when the fish didn't show up. Actually, most of the time, the fish didn't show up. Fishing and catching fish are not the same. It has been my experience that people who only like to catch fish rarely have a good time. In the end, they are always disappointed, and eventually, they stop fishing altogether.

After a few years, the seasons began to flow, and you started to see the patterns in nature, something the older kids seemed to know intuitively. You had to put in the time on the water. You had to participate. You had to be open and sensitive to the changes and the patterns above and below the water; the fish, the bait, the migrations of the birds, the winds, tides, rain, and of course, the daily thunderstorms. Mother Nature was sometimes at her best and sometimes at her worst, but once in tune, you always felt her presence. You had to learn to make the connections yourself, though; it wasn't something someone else could do for you.

It's a physical, mental, and spiritual connection I can't really explain. I can feel it on either side of the waterline and in the thunderstorms that should scare the crap out of you. One day, you find yourself on the end of the pier in the middle of a monster thunderstorm, protected by nothing more than a rain jacket and shorts thinking, *this is the coolest thing I've ever seen.*

You didn't just see it; you felt a part of it. Everything in nature is connected, but very few people experience the connection because, in our modern lives, we put so many barriers between ourselves and the raw forces of nature. When you are young, every day is a new experience physically and emotionally, and (hopefully) spiritually, in some sense. We were a tribe, and even though we would have never admitted it at the time, we needed each other.

We depended on each other for almost everything. We were getting older, and like most kids our age, we wanted to expand our horizons; we wanted to see what was around the corner and down the road—as long as the road followed the river or, at the very least, ended up at the river. We expected the fishing only to get better or, at least, excitingly different.

Some of the older kids ventured west, falling in love with the Intracoastal Waterway and the fabulous snook and tarpon fishing they found from the local bridges. Some were drawn by the legends of mammoth tarpon in the New River. Others fell in love with the man-made freshwater canals that crisscrossed Broward County, especially the brackish water canals provided by all the county dams, dikes, and spillways. In short, Broward and Palm Beach Counties beckoned with a treasure of incredible fishing spots.

Others went north to Pompano Pier, Dania Pier, Deerfield Pier, and eventually the pier that all piers are measured against, Lake Worth Pier. From there, some of the kids went even farther north to Sebastian Inlet; some of those never came back. Others again pushed south to the Florida Keys. It all depended on your mode of transportation. Mine happened to be a bicycle, which proved somewhat limiting.

Before it was ready for the trash heap, I had racked up as many miles on my trusty Schwinn ten-speed as any teenager could have put on his rundown, old car. The only downside to a bicycle was that it restricted the number of rods and the amount of gear you could carry.

Looking back now, I am amazed at how much fishing gear I managed to amass at such a young age. At any given time, I must have owned twenty to twenty-five (maybe even thirty) rods and one can only guess how many reels. Then there were the cast nets, bait buckets, live wells, coolers, tackle bags, and tackle boxes plus various surfboards in different lengths and shapes. I wish I could explain how and where it all came from or, even better yet, who paid for it all. I know we did well in selling our catch to the local restaurants that lined A1A at the time. A lot of the rods we built. In fact, my parents' garage looked more like a tackle shop and surf shop than it did a garage, and I hadn't even discovered fly-fishing yet.

My sister keeps telling me she thinks I probably had more than twenty surfboards in my parents' garage at one time or another. I don't remember owning that many, but it does sound like something I would do. Surfboards are like a vintage Holland & Holland. It's as much about the craftsmen as it is about the shotgun. Surfboards are as much about the shaper as they are about the board itself. Who in his right mind wouldn't want to own a few Lightning Bolts shaped by Gerry Lopez, "Mr. Pipeline" himself?

Some things are probably better left unanswered. I have to admit that the older kids and many of the retirees kept the local rats in stock. For a long time, most of my surfboards were hand-me-downs. I don't think I paid for a surfboard until I reached high school—then, I might have gone overboard.

When I look back at the quality fishing I was exposed to in the late sixties and the early seventies, I feel a wave of caution sweep over me—an inexplicable hesitation to tamper with the truth in fear that no one will believe me. Yet I need for people to believe me: I feel like I need to shout it from the highest rooftop! I need people to understand what was and what will never be again. Of course, it's also a matter of perspective; even when I was growing up on Anglin's Pier, the old-timers were already complaining about the decline in fishing.

They complained about everything: rock and roll, long hair, the kids surfing in and out of the pilings, the absence of bait, the scarcity of fish, the overabundance of tourists, the quality of the food at the diner, and always about the pier rats and all our fishing gear scattered from one end of the pier to the other. Eventually, we stopped listening. Still, the old-timers were always kind to us. In some weird way, I think they felt responsible for us. As a kid, I could never understand how anyone could complain about the fishing. Today, I realize that the fishing could never have been as good as the fishing was when the old-timers had been youngsters themselves.

The early seventies also was the time when my parents pulled the plug on Lauderdale by the Sea and moved—again. They liked to move a lot, never too far, but just far enough for me to have to change schools. In fact, I am not sure I ever attended the same school for two years in a row. In some ways, I was lucky that, in the early seventies, Fort Lauderdale remained reasonably small, at least what I considered small. There was green space between Dania and Miami, and Pompano and Palm Beach to the north, although Fort Lauderdale had been pushing to the west since the 1920s. West Davie was virtually made up of cowboys and cow pastures. Most of the man-made canals were still undeveloped. That's not to say that we didn't see development coming, but it's safe to say, we didn't understand it. In the years to come, though, we watched the wave of humanity wash over South Florida like a tsunami.

During our time, Fort Lauderdale quickly turned into a maze of canals; most of them—especially the ones close to the beaches—came equipped with shiny new concrete seawalls. It was only a matter of time before the walls started closing in. South Florida had survived Flagler and his damn railroad. Then came the land boom of the 1920s that took advantage of the damming, diking, and filling in of the Everglades. (Actually, the assault on the Everglades had started even earlier, in the late 1800s. Even then, the bastards starting chopping down the hardwood hammocks and, as the technology improved, took everything—and I mean everything. In essence, that was the beginning of the end of South Florida.)

The second major land boom, following World War II, rocked the state to its foundations. In 1972, Florida was about to get crushed again. This time it would be devastating: an even greater exodus from the collapsed cities of the northeastern states was headed our way. South Florida would never be the same again.

• 3 •

Go West, Young Man

It doesn't matter how old you are: exploring is exploring, and some people were born to push the limits. It can be a lesson hard learned, but more often than not, the harder you push, the bigger the rewards and, of course, the more significant the risk. The problem is that the rewards are rarely what you thought they would be, and sometimes, or I should say most of the time, you don't recognize them until later in life. When you are young, you crave instant satisfaction; young fishermen like big fish, as many of them as they can catch. It's human nature, and absolutely nothing is wrong with it. In fact, I would say that the majority of the kids who grew up on Anglin's Pier had more experience hooking, fighting, and landing big fish before they were old enough to drive than the majority of today's fishermen could ever imagine or even comprehend. The quality and growth of a young angler has always been predicated on the amount of time he or she can spend on the water and, of course, the quality of the resources.

In the early seventies, we had the run of all the beaches from Palm Beach to North Biscayne Bay. Most of the condominiums and apartment complexes tended to be on the west side of A1A; the beachside was left open, so you could pull over and park just about anywhere. By this time, we had been fishing the beaches and the piers for three or four years. Some of the older kids had been fishing Anglin's Pier since the early 1960s. Of course, I wouldn't necessarily call them kids anymore, regardless of how they acted. I use the moniker "kids" more in reference to our youthful exuberance than our age. Immaturity (or degeneracy) aside, nobody knew South Florida's waters and fishing patterns better than we did. Of course, that's a canard of sorts, and maybe a little delusional, but we were young and full of piss and vinegar; we were masters of own domain.

9

I wouldn't exactly say we had it down pat, but we were tuned into the seasons and even the micro patterns within the individual seasons. We were growing older, and we needed to explore. It seemed like we were discovering new fisheries every day. Of course, the new places we fished had been fished for a long time, but they were new to us, and that's all that counted. Later in life, I would tell anyone who would listen that if you ran across a ditch or a small pond in South Florida that held water year-round, you had to stop and fish it. More often than not, it probably held fish of some kind, sometimes a lot of fish. You would be amazed at the number of small tarpon and snook I have caught in what the state called mosquito ditches: nothing more than minor drainages that ran into larger creeks that, in themselves, were nothing but tributaries to a more substantial man-made canal.

In 1964, in an attempt to control, or at the very least, curb the mosquito population, the county water districts started digging or laying pipe to drain the wetlands. The goal was safeguarding tourists and snowbirds from the local vampires. I don't know if it was intentional or accidental, but the county water districts created a discrete, and oftentimes hard to find, tarpon fishery. I doubt that it was intentional because the local, county, or state governments have always done the opposite of what would have been best for the fisherman. Still, for whatever reason, they created a much-needed nursery for juvenile tarpon and snook.

My parents had never visited any relatives, much less taken a vacation of any kind. Then one day, out of the blue, they decided to visit my aunt and uncle in Tampa—relatives I had only met once, years earlier, and whose names or appearance I could no longer recall. Why were we going just then? I have no idea. But, to get there, we had to cross the Everglades. After many years of hearing outrageous stories about the wildlife and the fishing in the Everglades and Ten Thousand Islands, I couldn't wait. I was salivating at the chance to fish either Alligator Alley or the Tamiami Canal.

I wanted to take everything: fishing rods, tackle boxes, cast nets, and coolers. Alligator Alley was a long, two-lane road that must have scared the crap out of snowbirds. The Everglades held little draw for most tourists. On the one hand, it must have been painfully dull; after all, it offered nothing to look at but swampland in all directions. It's for damn sure, no civilization-loving snowbird wanted to stop there. On the other hand, it was terrifying, muggy, hot, and full of mosquitoes. Those few brave souls who did halt rarely stayed outside their vehicles for very long. For years, people have pushed through one of the most incredible ecosystems on the planet at eighty miles an hour, securely cocooned in air-conditioned automobiles. If you want to call yourself a fisherman or a naturalist, though, you have to leave the contraption behind: you have to walk, or crawl, or swim some. You have to pay a little blood tribute to the mosquitoes, skirt a few gators, and shriek at a few snakes.

Like many natural ecosystems in Florida, the Everglades were (and still are) reviled by most but loved by a few. Other than the white, sandy beaches that make up the majority of the Florida coastline—and maybe that out-of-control monstrous conglomeration in the middle of the state called Orlando—few aspects of Florida seem attractive to most visitors. The land that remains has always been considered a resource to be devoured and consumed by developers. It's been raped repeatedly since the Spanish first landed in 1513 looking for gold. The British soon followed the Spanish, then the Spanish again, punctuated by a short stint by the French, until, eventually, East and West Florida were purchased by the United States. At one time, West Florida's state line went all the way to the Mississippi River. That changed drastically with the purchase of the Louisiana Territory.

My family formed no exception to avoiding the raw side of Florida. Although I had lived in Florida most of my childhood, I had never seen Alligator Alley. I had heard of it, though, and found the stories hard to believe. Thursday morning, the day of our trip, finally arrived. We left just before sunrise and sort of drifted west. It didn't take long for me to figure out that my stepfather didn't have a clue where he was going, although it really wasn't rocket science: all you had to do was go west. When you couldn't go in that direction any farther without drowning, you had to turn either right or left, depending on whether you found yourself north or south of the Alley. Despite my stepfather's navigational challenges, we finally located the Alley's tollbooth and coughed up the obligatory seventy-five cents. I doubt they collected enough money in a week to pay the attendants but hope that the budget at least provided enough mosquito repellent.

Alligator Alley was considered a death trap at the time. The American Automotive Association begged folks to avoid it like the plague. At one time, it was considered one of the most dangerous roads in America. The official name was not even Alligator Alley; it was named the Everglades Parkway, but the official name never stuck. Hampton Dunn gets the lion's share of credit for naming the new road Alligator Alley. An old curmudgeon by the name of Guy Stovall is credited with pushing the building project through and finally completing the massive job. No rest stops, service stations, lights of any kind existed along the Alley at the time. Luckily, the people working the tollbooth always allowed you to turn around and go back to where you came from.

On the side of the tollbooth in Andytown, going east, a substantial wooden sign listed all of the deadly animals native to the Glades—including the birds of prey. Alligator Alley truly was wild: gators loomed everywhere you looked; the Florida panther made its home there; immense herds of wild boar roamed the Florida Everglades at will, and snakes of all description hid in perforated limestone holes trying to keep cool. If you dared to leave the safety of your car and spend a few minutes looking at the ground, you probably discovered you were standing on one.

The Alley primarily sits on a combination of the Biscayne Aquifer and the Floridian aquifer; thus, the ground consists of porous limestone with a multitude of holes and cavities that run throughout the aquifers. Alligator Alley traverses the upper regions of what is now Everglades National Park. The park encompasses not only the Florida Everglades, but also includes the Big Cypress country, the Mangrove Coast, the Ten Thousand Islands, the Cape Sable region, and Florida Bay. Everglades National Park consists of more than a million acres and is the third largest park in the nation. Before the Army Corp of Engineers started cutting, damming, diking, and draining the Everglades for developers, tourists, and farmers, the Everglades covered more than seven million acres in five Florida counties.

During our maiden voyage through it, I convinced my stepfather to pull over at the second homemade boat ramp we came to—though I use the term "boat ramp" loosely. We soon learned that we should have brought a case of mosquito repellent. One can of Off for the entire family didn't cut it—the mosquitoes just laughed at us.

When I was in elementary school, Broward County would fly old C140s low over the treetops to spray malathion laced with various amounts of DDT on the kids waiting for the school bus. It was one step short of Agent Orange. This regular dousing forms a convenient excuse for any senior moments or lapses in judgment later in life. Leaving that aside, even if I could have called in a napalm strike that day on the Alley, I am not sure it would have been enough. The mosquitoes were as thick as molasses.

I remember staring into the canal that ran parallel along the Alley. The water ran so clear you could see the brown and green algae that grow around the roots on the cattails—you could almost count the individual strands. It was one of cleanest, if not the cleanest, watershed I have ever seen, and probably the most pristine fishery. Encouraged, I ran back to the car and grabbed a loaf of old bread that I had brought from home. Rolling the bread in my hands, I turned it into as many crumbles as I could. When I pitched the crumbles into the canal, it took only a few minutes before the water boiled with bluegills of all sizes, joined by some of the largest wild shiners I had ever seen. A few minutes later, the bass showed up and started chasing the shiners. Some of the bass blew up right at my feet. It felt like staring into one of the saltwater tanks at the Miami Seaquarium. I couldn't stop gaping at all the fish—then I saw two rather large gators on the other side of the canal slide down the grassy bank into the water and disappear. Creating a frenzy of fish in gator country has the same effect as tempting a young kitten with a rubber mouse on a string—the gators could ignore the temptation for just so long.

At that stage, my mother rolled down the window and screamed at me to get back in the car, or they would leave me. Looking back, I wish they had left me there with my fishing gear (and maybe some food, water, and bug repellent). Despite the additional incentive of gators on the move, I don't remember jumping right back into the car. I sort of slowly backed up to my stepfather's rusted-out Ford Falcon. Also, I can't say for sure whether my mother was more interested in getting away from the mosquitoes or preventing her one and only son from getting mauled.

Years later, I would learn to love the big lizards and what they mean to the Everglades. Like most animals, especially the ones that tend to look threatening, gators eventually were pushed to the brink of extinction. Thus, the American alligator found itself on the Endangered Species list. Through persistence and proper management, the species has made a tremendous comeback. Unfortunately, they belong to a relatively exclusive club in that respect; few animal or plant species ever make it off the Endangered Species list.

• *4* •

The River of Grass

*M*y first family vacation didn't last long; and, for some strange reason, we didn't come back via the Alley but via the relatively new Florida Turnpike. Canals lined both sides of the turnpike, and the occasional lake graced an exit. Everywhere you looked you saw wading birds, shore birds, redwing blackbirds, and a few ducks. From what l could see, fish were rising everywhere. I learned years later that virtually anywhere you dig for fill for new roads in South Florida, you end up with a canal or lake, which eventually ends up filled with fish and birds. I can only assume that the birds came first and transplanted fish eggs from watershed to watershed.

Once we made it back to Fort Lauderdale, I kept pestering my older friends to fish the Glades with me, especially those who possessed a driver's license and occasional access to parental vehicles. Of course, I later discovered access and permission meant two different things, but I digress.

Fishing in the Everglades wasn't really new when I first thought of it, of course. The Calusa had been making a living on the edge of the Everglades for maybe two thousand years or longer. Our excursions were different in that the state of Florida had built a shiny new road right through the middle of the Everglades. In some ways, it was like a pier along the Atlantic Ocean. You could drive up and down the road and pull off anywhere you wanted to and fish.

We even started camping on the Alley, especially in the winter when the mosquitoes thinned out. When we knew that we were going to fish the Alley for any length of time, we hung our jeans, long-sleeved shirts, and baseball caps on the clothesline behind the house. Then, we sprayed our clothes with the insect repellent Backwoods Off. Years later, when Cutters came out, we switched because Cutters contained a higher concentration of DEET.

Sometimes, we coated our clothes twice. Then, when we jumped out of the car on the Alley, we covered ourselves again. I remember spraying myself so many times with Cutters, I started vomiting violently. I know what you are thinking—we were nuts. But who knows? Maybe we were a little off plumb.

After a few years, we started dragging canoes and old worn-out john-boats to the Alley. Some of the johnboats were in such bad shape, the bottoms were held together with screws and epoxy. And, yes, they still leaked a little—sometimes more than just a little. Thank goodness for our old-fashioned bilge pump. If I remember right, Clorox made it.

Our canoes tended to be in better shape than the johnboats, even though we thought it prudent always to keep several rolls of duct tape handy. I still remember my first canoe: it was a hand-me-down from my next-door neighbor, Steve Harris. Once we could lay claim to transportation up and down the Alley, we started venturing into the backcountry. The water usually reached several feet above the winter flows in the summer because, yes, the Everglades do flow. However, water primarily flows over the Glades like a sheet of glass. So, it depended on the season and the amount of rain how many miles we could venture into the backcountry north or south of the Alley. Unlike the Tamiami Canal that crosses the Everglades farther south, the water runs fresh north and south of Alligator Alley. I didn't know it at the time, but the water was controlled farther north but south of Lake Okeechobee. My "pristine" fishery was managed by something called the South Florida Water Management District.

Along the Alley, we fished for bass and bluegill, but the Glades also teemed with giant prehistoric gar, and every once in a blue moon, we would catch a chain pickerel or two. On a good morning, we could catch eighty, ninety, maybe a hundred bass (as I said above: gluttony, the sin of youth). Most of the bass weighed between one and two pounds, but we caught more than our share of four- and five-pound fish on wild shiners. When the bass were bedding in the spring, we would land a few fish every year that pushed the scales to six or seven pounds. The bass and bluegills were always in great shape—you never landed one with parasites or fungus. It also helped that, in the early days, you rarely ran into anybody fishing the Alley.

In the mornings, we threw topwater baits. When the sun caught fire, and the plants started wilting, we mainly fished with rubber worms or the occasional crankbait. We swatted mosquitoes and did our best to avoid the fire ants. It's surprising how much self-inflicted pain you can endure when you are a kid: wind and rain, heat and humidity, and mosquitoes and fire ants didn't seem to bother us too much. If it got too hot, you just took off your flip-flops and T-shirts and jumped into the water. I know what you're thinking: what happened to the snakes and gators? Somehow, we survived.

That's another thing about being young and stupid. I can only say that when I was a kid, I used to spend a lot of time at the Hall of Fame pool in Fort Lauderdale, where Johnny Weissmuller was one of the founders, the chairman of the board, and an occasional lifeguard. So, if Tarzan could wrestle alligators and crocodiles and live, why couldn't we? Years later, I found out that the Tarzan movies were filmed in Silver Springs, and the rubber alligators and crocodiles were not very ferocious.

The difference between the summer and the winter in the Glades is subtle. Fishing changes some because of the cooler nights and the milder days, but not as much as one might think. If the winter flows were low, the fish would stay in the deeper holes; if the waters were extremely low, fish would concentrate in the backcountry in gator holes. The low or high flow didn't necessarily mean the water table went up or down, nor did it dictate what season it was. Flow didn't depend much on summer or winter: it was probably the South Florida Water Management District delivering whatever the sugarcane and the citrus industry needed. It reminds me of a famous line from *Casablanca*, when Rick rags on Ugarte for selling exit visas:

"I don't mind a parasite; I object to a cut-rate one."

"Rick, look at all the unfortunate people I help."

"For a price, Ugarte—for a price."

The Everglades have never been managed for the sake of the Glades or its wildlife, let alone the fisheries. They're managed to line the pockets of the South Florida Water Management District commissioners. Water always went to the highest bidder and probably still does. Always follow the money or, in this case, the lobbyists and the politicians—everybody had their hands out.

· *5* ·

The Mythical Waterfall

*M*eanwhile, at the pier, life changed. New kids were showing up, and some of the older kids, now teenagers, discovered girls, which dampened their commitment to fishing and surfing. The new runts were different and, at times, challenging to manage. They didn't understand the pier hierarchy. I have no idea who pinned the name *runts* on the new kids, but it stuck and seemed damned appropriate at the time. The new kids didn't seem as gullible as we had been, and even worse, they always seemed to have money, which made them downright belligerent.

When we wanted something from the tackle shop or the little diner, they were supposed to hop to it and not bitch about it. I have a close friend who ordered two hamburgers, an order of fries, a milkshake, and two dozen live shrimp from the tackle shop; he gave the kid two dollars and told him to make sure he brought back the change. Maybe we were a little rough on the new kids, but where do you think we got the ideas in the first place? We paid our dues. Now it was their turn. From what I can remember, life always runs downhill.

The runts had their benefits, too; one of them kept telling us about the canal he lived on and all the snook and tarpon his dad kept catching. Supposedly, the canal terminated in, of all things, a waterfall. Then one night, when his dad picked him up, we asked about this mythical "waterfall."

How can you have a waterfall in a state as flat as an ironing board? It turned out to be a spillway. OK, what the hell is a spillway? I lived on the same canal with the spillway. Did I mention that we had moved again? We now lived on the Cypress Creek Canal. The canal served as the border between Fort Lauderdale and Pompano Beach. According to Ron, the kid's dad, Cypress Creek Canal in West Broward, where I lived, was very fresh

19

and contained plenty of tarpon. Ron invited us over for dinner that night and afterward promised to show us how to fish the spillway.

When we pulled up to the spillway, so much water was blowing over the top we could hardly hear ourselves think. It had been raining for days, and it didn't look like it would stop anytime soon. Thousands of gallons of water flowing over the top created an enormous amount of whitewater and foam. You could hardly see the water beneath!

The spillway sat at the junction where Cypress Creek dumped into one of the saltwater drainage canals that flowed into Lake Santa Barbara. Eventually, it ran into the Intracoastal Waterway and from there into the Atlantic Ocean. In theory, you could catch anything on the saltwater side and, over the next few years, we did. We caught huge snook below the spillway and rather large tarpon on the freshwater side. At one time, one of the kids managed to break the IGFA record for the largest cubera snapper on twenty-pound test. The record didn't last long, but still.

Silver mullet tended to congregate in the brackish water below the spillway. On the downside of the spillway—the saltwater side—two long seawalls gave way to a pile of limestone rubble that the city had put in place to prevent erosion during heavy storms. The chain-link fence protecting the spillway looked more like a prison. Spools of industrial-strength barbed wire lined the top of the fence like candy cane. I guess the city threw down the gauntlet and challenged us to find our way in. The spillway had a boardwalk and handrail going across the top, so the engineers could do what engineers do. My thoughts were, first, I didn't bring enough gear; and second, how do I get to the other side of the fence and then to the top of the spillway?

The canal teemed with silver mullet, and on the right tide enormous schools of jack crevalle came through, ravaging the mullet and everything else in sight. The jacks were massive and incredibly aggressive; at times, we were afraid to get near the water. Away from the spillway, the jacks would blow the mullet up on the beach; all you had to do was walk down the beach and pick the mullet out of the red mangrove roots. One morning, I think I lost seven Zara Spooks in a row to big jacks. Eventually, I had to quit fishing because I didn't have any line left on my Penn 710 spinning reel.

It was paradise. Most of the spillways we fished as kids are still around and probably somewhat productive. As productive as they were when we were kids? Not in a million years! Ron, always the law-abiding father, claimed not to have any idea how to traverse the fence, or if he did, he wasn't going to show us and certainly wasn't going to give his son any crazy ideas. That meant we had to find our own way through, which came later. For the next several hours, we pitched red and white 52m11 Mirrolures and a few Zara Spooks into the heavy water that blew over the top of the spillway from the rocks below—not the best way to fish the spillway, but we did catch a few snook that night. Before we left,

I jumped a nice tarpon that politely swam away with my Mirrolure. You laugh, but when I was a kid, Mirrolures were expensive.

In some ways, spillways are a paradox, although I have to admit, I loved spillway fishing and have caught some amazing fish there. If water flowing is over the top for any length of time, the fishing can be cosmic. The problem is, spillways exist to drain the wetlands behind them. The state digs canals, then drains the water into a saltwater tributary. Afterward, the water runs into an estuary or the Intracoastal Waterway and eventually into the ocean.

The state does this for one reason: to create dry land for development or farmland. Farmland sounds quaint, but large-scale industries such as sugar, citrus, and cattle of South Florida have huge, deleterious effects on the surrounding ecosystems. Creating farmable land means losing the precious wetlands that replenish our aquifers, the main reason why we have lost more than six million acres of wetlands since the turn of the century. That is a loss for which we can thank our state and local governments plus every city council and zoning board in South Florida.

Whenever someone, such as a local environmental group, decides enough is enough, they can either sue the government or effect the inclusion of a referendum on a ballot to stop draining the wetlands. Sadly, in the end, the referenda are always defeated. The wetlands never win. The water needed to replenish the Everglades and provide fresh water to the mangrove islands and estuaries of the Ten Thousand Islands is diverted, so the snowbirds from the Northeast and Midwest can have their second or third winter home.

· 6 ·

The Abilene Paradox

If you hang around the same group of kids long enough, you become a tribe. You start to dress alike, sound alike, and act alike. The tribal members adopt the same stories, vernacular, mannerisms, and, in some cases, the same haircuts. Adopting a herd mentality, everyone starts to think alike. That's when it gets a little spooky. The downside to all the conformity is that it eventually reaches the point where you can easily talk the herd into just about anything. But, of course, anyone who's been a teenager may know that "anything" doesn't necessarily mean legal.

Years later, I discovered that psychologists refer to this as the Abilene Paradox. A group of people collectively decides on a course of action that is counter to the preferences of many or all of the individuals in the group. That was us—we were the walking, talking definition of the Abilene Paradox.

I have no idea why we kept moving. We hated to fish in any one place for very long. If it wasn't productive, we kept trucking. We moved from pier to beach to riding our bicycles in and out of neighborhoods scoping out possible fishing spots. We were always looking for new ways to access places where we weren't supposed to be in the first place. Some might call it mischief or lack of parental oversight. Then again, it might just be called being a kid intent on having fun.

Against this backdrop, we had our own youthful mission of a dubious nature: how to traverse that fence at the Cypress Creek Canal spillway, even though several corroded signs bolted to the fence warned, "This property was owned and managed by the Broward County Water District, and trespassers will be prosecuted."

We needed to be on top of the spillway. Because we had grown up on Anglin's Pier, experience had taught us that if you wanted to pitch live bait, it's easier and better to be above the bait to have more control. Unfortunately, the fence was built like a medieval fortress. Breaching it would take serious tools and a little backbone. At this point, a little ingenuity or common sense might have gone a long way. Unfortunately, we were not yet thus endowed.

Privacy was hard to come by. The spillway proved popular: people showed up with five-gallon buckets, four or five cane poles, and three or four loaves of bread to spend all day fishing for mullet. Armed with a bobber and snatch hook, they wetted the white bread and plastered it around the shank of the snatch hook. When the mullet started nibbling on the bread, the bobber started bouncing up and down, and they lifted the cane pole straight up and snagged the mullet in the lower lip. The first time I saw someone do this, I was dumbfounded. It was the most ingenious thing I had ever witnessed.

Fascinating as it was, all these people milling around our intended crime scene made us a little nervous. On the upside, a two-lane dirt road ran parallel to the canal. If any real threat emerged, we had a quick exit—unless, we weren't paying attention and ended up with the water as our only practical escape route. That scenario lacked appeal, not least because it prevented us from taking our fishing gear with us.

Clever miscreants that we prided ourselves to be, we sure scouted a lot. I can't tell you how many times we rode our bicycles down that dirt road to conquer that fence and never even once made an attempt. The fence became our Mount Everest; we had made it to base camp, but instead of climbing, we stood around and came up with endless reasons why not to climb over or scurry beneath the fence. Some might call it procrastination; we preferred to think of it as due diligence. It did occur to us that if we told the police officer someone else had cut the hole in the fence and offered him a snook (as a gift, you understand, not a bribe), our chances of getting away with a warning improved. A ten- to fifteen-pound snook goes a long way when you have "the man" breathing down your neck. If "the man" happens to be a woman—forget it. Your ass is fried.

The fence remained intact until one Saturday morning. I sneaked out of the house before my parents woke up, grabbed a few rods and a five-gallon bucket, jumped on my bicycle, and worked my way down to the spillway before sunrise. If I was lucky, I might catch a few snook, or maybe jump an early morning tarpon, before heading down to Anglin's Pier to check out the surf. If nothing else, I could hang out at the pier all day or maybe all weekend if the surf was up. I kept several pairs of shorts, swim trunks, and a few T-shirts in the two lockers I rented on the pier for this purpose. On this particular Saturday, I arrived at the spillway before the mullet fishermen. Still, several guys were working the beachside pitching plugs. Even back then, the good spots were always crowded. People can't keep their mouths shut.

As soon as someone discovers a great fishing spot, the whole world has to be informed, until all of the good spots are gone.

About to cave and start the long bike ride to Anglin's Pier, I noticed a bright orange Datsun pickup barreling down the two-lane dirt road that led to the spillway. It looked like one of the small, orange trucks used in the pool cleaning business. From what I could see, the whole truck appeared to be held together with baling wire. Little remained of the fender wells; the door panels sported patches of Bondo, and the tires looked like they had seen better days. What drew my attention most were all the rods hanging out of the passenger-side window. The driver had rolled down both windows and, although he displayed some skill at missing the deepest potholes filled with rainwater, everything in the cab was getting thoroughly drenched.

A few seconds later, the small truck veered off the road and disappeared into a large stand of black mangroves behind the spillway. I had no idea what prompted the off-road antics—it wasn't illegal to park here—not that I knew anyway. I waited to see what would happen next. When I didn't see car or driver reemerge, I grew curious and meandered up the road to see where the truck had ended up. If the driver had been injured or killed, someone would have to call for help—and take care of his fishing gear, right?

Full of such good-Samaritan thoughts, I walked up behind the orange truck as if making my way up to the main road. My attempts at playing coy ended abruptly when I reached the truck: the amount of tackle stuffed into that small vehicle floored me. Even though the bed was almost completely rusted out, it carried countless five-gallon buckets, Styrofoam coolers, and what looked like old commercial nets—plus two spare tires. Cast nets of all shapes and sizes, a dip net, and a raggedy old seine net that stunk to high heaven rounded out the still life.

When the door to the truck opened, it basically fell off its hinges. A young guy with a long beard stepped out, tying his hair into a ponytail. He didn't look like much. In fact, I thought he probably lived in the old truck—a notion reinforced by the sleeping bag rolled up in the front seat. But his tackle appeared in great shape, so he couldn't be all bad.

The guy ignored me at first—he might have said something, but I don't remember. I was still trying to act rather nonchalant about the whole thing, as if I wasn't dying to find out what he was going to do next. Not paying me much heed, he grabbed one of the buckets, then lifted one of the cast nets over the tailgate. The lead line at the bottom of the net made a sound as if a load of rocks had been dumped into the truck bed. I watched him take the bucket and cast net down to the water and crawl over the mangrove roots. After he'd filled the bucket with water, he looked back at me and asked if I wanted to carry the bucket. I jumped in and followed him down the canal: a friendship was born.

After a while, my mysterious new friend stopped, folded the net into two halves, threw it over his left shoulder, and put the lead line into his mouth. He hunched down, twisted, and threw the net forward into the air. It opened into a perfect circle. I was impressed—I had been throwing a cast net for years, and mine never opened in a perfect circle. In my defense, I was much smaller at the time. By the time I waded into the water up to my knees, there wasn't much room left above the water line.

In any event, his net hit the water, then sank to the bottom like a rock. When he pulled on the rope and dragged the net up onto the beach, he was able to shake eighteen to twenty finger mullet into his bucket, meaning we were ready—for what, I had no idea. I assumed we were going to fish on the same pile of rubble I hated so much. Pete (his name, as I found out later) grabbed the net. I lugged the bucket. Back at the truck, he threw the net into the bed and grabbed a tarpon rod. What he pulled out next proved interesting: he reached into the toolbox on the floorboard and armed himself with a pair of wire cutters.

I snatched my spinning rod with one hand, the bucket with the other, and followed as quickly as I could without spilling the water from the bucket. Slowing my progress, the finger mullet kept jumping out of the bucket. By the time we reached the spillway, the two guys pitching plugs had gone home, or at least someplace else. I started scampering over to my spot on the rubble when I looked back and saw my new buddy headed toward the fence. I tried to catch up, but every time I picked up speed, another finger mullet went airborne. When at last I made it to the fence, I found my partner in crime cutting a hole. Once it was big enough for him to fit, he threw his rod through, then followed it, and reached back for the bucket, laughing.

By that time, I finally got up the courage to ask him his name—he looked back, laughed again, and said, "Pete Stroble." Hell, he seemed all right, even though he kept laughing. At first, I thought he must have been a bit high. Later, I thought he was a little "touched"—you know, a little crazy probably came closer to the truth. He told me that before I sneaked through the fence, I had better understand that we had just broken the law and, if we were caught, we would receive a ticket, if not go to jail. I reminded him that *we* hadn't broken the law; he had.

"I am just an innocent kid who just happened to be here."

· 7 ·

Partners in Crime

*T*hrough the fence, I went: down the road of crime. And for what, I kept asking myself. A snook? Well, if nothing else, by the end of the day, I would be a local hero—or an inmate at the Broward County lockup. Like Alice, I went down the rabbit hole, even though I wasn't old enough to know who Alice was.

I followed Pete to the top of the spillway. I was excited—and protected by youthful inexperience from fully understanding the consequences of what I had just participated in. It was the first time I had ever been on top of the spillway; maneuvering it felt a little edgy. The boardwalk that crossed the top of the spillway was only twelve- to eighteen-inches wide and cleared the roaring water right below by only two or three feet. The rush of water boiling over into the saltwater canal made a lot of angry noise.

When I put down the bucket, Pete hooked an eight-inch finger mullet through the lips. Then he backed off on the reel, put the Jigmaster in free spool, and pitched the mullet into the foam right below our feet. The finger mullet wasn't in the water for more than ten seconds before a sixteen- or eighteen-pound snook flashed and swallowed it. Pete put the reel in gear, came tight, and reared back—setting the hook. Minutes later, the fish lay on the grass beside the spillway. I kept thinking, *Is it really that easy?*

Pete caught three more snook within the next twenty minutes, which prompted him to pack up. He was getting ready to dump the remaining finger mullet back into the water when I screamed.

"What are you doing?"

Here, he was on his way home, and I hadn't had a chance to try. I had shared all the work, carried the bucket of finger mullet—I was even a coconspirator in crime, and I wanted to catch a snook. I think Pete could see I was a little off-kilter at that moment. He told me I could keep the remainder of the finger mullet, if I really wanted them. I remember telling him he had to stay with me until I caught a few snook, and we would leave together, partners in crime, so to speak. If we did get caught, I was going to blame everything on Pete.

Good-naturedly, Pete took over the role of guide for the next ten minutes or so. It didn't take long before I had hooked and landed several nice fish: one right after another. Incredible how easy it was. A little later, I carried the snook and all my tackle back through the fence. By that time, Pete had driven his truck up to the fence. While I loaded our gear, Pete repaired the fence. The guy was brilliant. Pete had brought a small roll of baling wire, which he used to tie the fence back together. He deposited my bike in the bed of his glorious, orange rust-bucket, and we headed off to the pier to have breakfast at the local diner and clean our snook.

Over the years, Pete and I repeated this crime many times at spillways from Palm Beach to Miami and from Naples to Sarasota. Luckily, we were never thrown in the hoosegow. We were questioned many times, also asked—or politely told—to leave and never come back, but we were never arrested. In some ways, the excitement of sneaking in and out of the spillways without being caught was as much fun as catching the fish.

The tough part about our nighttime shenanigans was that we needed to keep it as quiet as possible. I could only assume that meant not telling the rest of the pier rats about the spillway. Of course, the tribe would have found out one way or another. If I told them about Pete, then Pete would probably get pissed. Life is full of tough decisions, but in the end everyone knew about the spillway and the fence anyway. So, I confessed, then admitted what we had done and how good the fishing was from the top of the spillway. In the end, I had to spill the beans to Pete. Fortunately, Pete seemed to care less whether or not they knew. Then again, loose lips do sink ships. Some things in life you should not share with your chatty friends. All that being said—without Pete and his trusty wire cutters and roll of baling wire, we couldn't have gotten through the fence regardless of how hard we tried.

Even though I am more than sure that many fishermen up and down the coast did the exact same thing—probably years before we did, or should I say at least before I did, Pete excelled at the game. I doubt the Cypress Creek was the first spillway he cut his way into. I mean, who brings a roll of baling wire to patch a fence? That takes some forethought and experience. I fished with Pete off and on over the next thirty years. Pete was a great friend and an important mentor, even if he continually laughed at me like a hyena.

To this day, I am not sure that Pete wasn't a little "touched." I could write a book about Pete alone, though I doubt if anybody would believe half of it. As time went by, we started fishing lots of spillways and drainage ditches—virtually anywhere the fresh meets the salt. You didn't have to be Albert Einstein to understand that there was something cosmic about the intersection between sweet and brine. Not all spillways were fenced in, or furnished a platform across their top. Some spillways are permanent dams. Some spillways also work as pumping stations.

I have read that South Florida boasts more than three thousand miles of canals and more than two thousand miles of levees. For the most part, the fixed dams tend to be open to the public, and no one really cares if you fish there. Some are even banked by parks with picnic tables; most are furnished with access roads. On the flip side, the number of people who fish the dams at any given time can be staggering, especially when it's been raining for several days. The fish tend to congregate in the tail out below the dam. I've heard many hypotheses over the years about why fish gather under spillways. Personally, I think snook and tarpon love the colder, highly oxygenated water. I know that's a simplistic answer, but sometimes the most straightforward conjecture is the best. In any event, rain and moving water are key.

• 8 •

Moving Water

To this day, I still can't drive through the Everglades without continually looking for moving water. When the water is high and running reasonably well, you can drive along the Tamiami Canal, especially near Chokoloskee and Everglades City, and see water pouring out of the sawgrass. In certain areas, it looks like a small tributary. Even from the road, you can usually spot the high water flowing through the sawgrass because of all the foam it churns up. Not technically tributaries, what you see are paths in the sawgrass that are only flushed when the water starts ripping.

Running water always takes the path of least resistance. This would be a great time to stop the car, relax by the sawgrass, and let the fish come to you. Take your time. Part of the allure of fishing is to slow down to a more natural, primordial pace. So many times, I have seen people jump out of the car, take twenty seconds to look around or, rather, take pictures to show off later, then dart back to the car and speed away. Exert some patience, unwind, and give the fish time to show themselves. That way, even if the fish don't show, you haven't "lost time" but gained inner peace that is likely to prolong your time on Earth. Hours spent meandering up and down riverbanks are rarely wasted. So many exciting and beautiful things are just waiting to be discovered by the person who bothers to look.

You could spend entire days stomping through the Glades and never see the same habitat twice. Some people might tell you the Everglades are monotonous. They could not be more wrong. That might be the impression to one who never bothers to get out of the car. Then again, the same can be said for most places: not much to see if you race through the landscape at eighty miles an hour.

For those who dare to explore, the smells and sounds of the Everglades are incredible. The more time you spend roaming, the more complex they

31

become. The fragrances can be musky at times because it is a swamp: it's as organic as it gets. It can be a complicated wallop of everything from flowers to swamp gas. Some people will tell you the Everglades stink, but I think they smell heavenly.

The sounds, too, are always multilayered. If you have the time to spend a few nights in the Glades, you might never be the same. Between the frogs, the insects, the gators, a panther screech or two, you might occasionally hear a black bear, and God only knows what else. It can be downright deafening. Snakes really don't make much noise—unless you happen to step on a rattlesnake—but people who encounter them do; they normally produce an interesting cacophony of squeals, screams, and curses. So, you might miss out on the subtle rattle itself.

In short, as yet, the Everglades suffer from no shortage of wildlife, though we certainly have lost a lot of diversity and gained some species that definitely do not belong. If you camp anywhere near Big Cypress National Preserve, you may even run into the Everglades version of Bigfoot, the Skunk Ape. I have never seen one, but I can't say that I've seen a Komodo dragon or a python, either. So, who knows? I have even seen the plaster mold of the Skunk Ape's footprint, proudly displayed at the Skunk Ape Research Head-quarters. Dave Shealy and his family were the first to see it; he believes in the Skunk Ape so much that he established a Skunk Ape Research Headquarters in Ochopee.

If you find yourself in Ochopee, Florida, stop and grab an official Skunk Ape T-shirt and mug. I can't say for certain that the Everglades are home to a species of humanoid ape unknown to modern science, but I can tell you for sure, they are home to many colorful characters that in themselves are worth a stop and a chat. In fact, you are reading a book written by someone who spent a considerable amount of time at the Bigfoot Headquarters on Mount Hood in Oregon. Maybe the evidence will convince you, or maybe the type of libation getting passed around the campfire will. Whether it is Boone's Farm apple wine or Mad Dog 2020 grape wine, a person can turn downright gullible after a bottle or two.

In my youth, though, I missed out on such libations. Not only were we too young to drink, but we also lacked acquaintances old enough and, maybe more to the point, dumb enough to buy it for us. That's my story, and I am sticking to it. I always thought, if you were old enough to camp in the Ever-glades, knowing that any minute you might be thrashed or spit-roasted over an open fire by the Skunk Ape, you were old enough to drink. Sometimes, staying in the Everglades at night simply called for a bit of liquid courage.

Returning to my original point, I know it sounds corny, but you have to slow down and become one with nature. Sometimes you can drive down the Alley and see fish everywhere, but that's not the norm. If you can't make heads or tails by looking at the water, the birds usually give it away. The Glades can be a great place to drag out your binoculars and marvel at the number of wading birds in one spot. You may have to hurry, though. Unfortunately for the wading birds, their reproduction has declined by as much as 90 percent for most species in the past century. The amount of water from Lake Okeechobee has been reduced so much that it has changed the hydrology of the Everglades, so much so that the majority of wading birds have had to alter their nesting habits.

Without enough fresh water or habitat along the coast, they have had to move inland, and that's changed their breeding cycle. It's the same old story; we knew it was happening, yet the National Park Service, the South Florida Water Management District, and the local and state governments did nothing to stop the insanity. Of course, you can't drain six million acres of wetlands, dam and dike Lake Okeechobee, dredge and straighten out the Kissimmee River, then pump runoff full of fertilizers, pesticides, and herbicides from the sugar and citrus industry into Lake Okeechobee and expect nothing to happen. To make things even worse, the majority of the toxic chemicals end up in the aquifers that supply the drinking water for Central and South Florida.

Obviously, it didn't move the needle of concern far enough because we all sat by and watched it happen, and it's still happening today. The big difference is that today it's exponentially worse, and the future looks dismal. It will only stop when people decide to manage nature for the sake of the environment and not merely for people. We have exceeded the carrying capacity of South Florida tenfold over the past century with no end in sight.

The population of the state of Florida has surpassed twenty-three million people, and the conservationists and environmentalists warn that another seventeen to twenty million people are headed this way over the next fifty years. Each year more than 140 million tourists visit the great state of Florida. Everyone wants to blame the politicians, but politicians don't drive policy—people drive policy, and politicians do what it takes to govern for four more years. It's all about growth and development. As Ed Abbey once said, "Growth and development is [sic] the ideology of the cancer cell."

In the end, we have no one to blame but ourselves. It's like being a Miami Dolphins fan—no matter how much we get down on our hands and knees and pray—Dan Marino will not run out of the locker room and save the day. George Washington Heyduke III will not HALO in from thirty thousand feet to make things right again. Each individual person must choose to leave a smaller footprint.

Is it truly necessary to plow down nature for yet another golf course, or a tennis court, located in a condominium complex only inhabited during three months of the year? Is it really necessary to build out instead of up? Is it really impossible to build roof gardens, to shade parking lots with solar-paneled roofs or trees? Is it really inconceivable to reduce, reuse, and recycle? How out of the question is it to champion good public transportation? Might it be time to support science and engineering with all our might, so that we may use as much energy as we need for our continual comfort and entertainment without polluting, slashing, and laying waste?

It's not too late. In some ways and in some places, the Everglades are still primordial. Also, nature is resilient; given a chance, it tends to bounce back. At times I would sit on the bank wondering what this place was like before the Spanish showed up and it still belonged to Paleo Indians, the Calusa, and eventually, the Seminoles. Mind you, if you were sitting there years before the Spanish arrived, you probably didn't have much leisure to wax philosophically and inhale inner peace, because it was a foregone conclusion that something or someone considered you dinner. Mother nature plays hardball to maintain a fragile balance. In less than a hundred years people—not government—have destroyed the balance and, with it, more than 70 percent of the wetlands. Ninety percent of the biomass in South Florida has disappeared.

Yet people keep coming by the millions. Even when I was young, the old folks lamented how much had been lost. We didn't see it because we didn't know any better, just like tourists today see more wildlife in Fort Lauderdale than they see in their inner cities and marvel at how biodiverse South Florida still is.

More often than not, when we found running water flowing out of the sawgrass, we caught snook, tarpon, largemouth bass, and even the occasional jack in the same tail outs without moving ten feet in either direction. They were usually smaller fish, but if they were around, they were always aggressive. We pitched micro baits such as small sinking Mirrolures and Rapala's swimming minnow. Then, years later when we started fly-fishing, we threw small Clouser minnows and deceivers—essentially, anything that mimicked a small baitfish. If you were good enough to throw the fly or plug back in the sawgrass and swim it out without it hanging up in the grass, you were almost always guaranteed a strike. The small tarpon were always hilarious. Sometimes they would jump so high and land so far back in the grass, we had to slide them out over the wet grass to get them back in the water—and hope we didn't draw the attention of the local gators.

Over the next several years we invested a tremendous amount of time and energy in paddling, hiking, camping, and driving in and out of the Everglades. It became an obsession with us. The problem with the Everglades is that everywhere you look, it looks fishy. You might be paddling down a creek thick with mangroves and mired in oyster bars; you might even see bait everywhere; you start to feel good about this creek, and then spend hours pounding the bank and never get a tug. Then you paddle into another creek or a tributary, not unlike the one you were just fishing, that basically feels dead. Suddenly, you see snook swimming in and out of the mangroves chasing baitfish or see huge redfish tailing on some mudflat that looks exactly like the mudflat you had just fished. Why? Who knows, but the fish know.

The Everglades can seem barren at times, and if you are trying to learn the ins and outs of one of the largest watersheds in the state by yourself, good luck. In the early years, we spent so much time fishing in places we thought were teeming with fish, without catching any, regardless of how many times we stopped and fished the same spots. The fish might have appeared on a different tide, or maybe on the same tide but at a different stage. It takes tremendous time and effort to even scratch the surface. To make things a little more interesting, the Glades are constantly changing, sometimes from day to day if not from tide to tide.

It's like putting together a jigsaw puzzle. When all the pieces are laid out on a table, it seems almost impossible. You start with the border or the corners because it makes sense. After all, you have an edge. The Everglades are essentially the same. You start at the edges where it seems to make more sense, and you are less likely to get lost, and then work your way inward. If you can afford it, the wisest move is to hire a guide for $600 a day and try to pay attention to where he takes you. Of course, that was never an option for us. More often than not, we had to scrape together our lunch money to help pay for the gas to get us to the Everglades. Like everyone else, we had to learn by trial and error, but we had a lot of fun doing it. In the end, the time and energy we invested paid huge dividends.

· 9 ·

My First Fly Rod

$\mathcal{I}$ had no idea what weight my fly rod was. Of course, at that time, the weight wouldn't have meant anything to me. The manufacturer's name was also conspicuous in its absence. Then again, I can't imagine a company putting its logo on that reel intentionally. It was a cheap piece of junk, a perfect fit for the rod. It didn't have a drag system or even a rudimentary click and paw. It was in such horrendous shape that I can only assume it had been dropped a few times or run over by a car or steamroller, possibly deliberately.

I only ended up with the rod in the first place because the previous owner had died. I have always wondered whether the rod had had sentimental value for him. Perhaps his father gave it to him on his tenth birthday—no one seemed to know much about the rod or the fisherman, or worse, even cared.

Travis invited me to join his newly minted fly-tying club that met on the second Thursday of every month in his garage. Travis was a local outdoor writer for the *Miami Herald*, and from what I had been told, he was one whale of a fly fisherman. I wasn't a fly fisherman at the time, but it sounded interesting, and I was game for pretty much anything that had to do with fishing. By the end of my first meeting, I managed to tie two of the ugliest flies tied by the hand of man. So, I walked out the door a fully equipped fly fisherman with a fly rod, a fly reel, and a cardboard box full of goodies that included the dead guy's vise, bobbins, and a few other tools and feathers. Believe it or not, I still have just about everything that was in the original box.

A few nights after my first fly-tying club meeting, I shattered it into a million pieces of fiberglass and tossed what was left of the rod, reel, and line into a campfire in the Everglades. It was safe to say that my foray into fly-fishing didn't have the "Splendid Splinter" shaking in his spikes. Because the one and only fly rod I owned had been incinerated during my last assault on the Everglades, my fly-fishing career was temporarily kaput. I amounted to nothing more than the run-of-the-mill neophyte. I didn't have the foggiest idea what I was doing. At that time, I knew so little about fly-fishing that I couldn't even formulate the right questions to ask or figure out to whom I should ask. I could only assume the path to enlightenment lay elsewhere.

Around that time, small fledging fly shops first started showing up on our radar, or at the least, it was the first time I started noticing them. Fly-fishing wasn't exactly brand-new in South Florida; it had been around for ages. Names such as Flip Pallot, Lefty Kreh, Steve Kantner, George Copeland, Billy Pate, Charles Waterman, A. J. McClane, and Stu Apte dominated the landscape. Quite a few tackle shops carried high-end fly rods and all the paraphernalia that went with them, but it all came at a price, one that few kids could afford.

I can remember the first time I saw someone using a fly rod on the pier. Several of the older kids were facing north and casting flies down current in less than two feet of water. They were barely on the pier, maybe thirty feet or so from the locker rack. If it had been a falling tide, there wouldn't have been any water to fish. Their fly rods were leaning up against the railing, and they had fifty or sixty feet of fly line curled up in a five-gallon bucket, which held several inches of water to keep the fly line wet. I knew Ron and Brandon from the pier, though I hadn't seen them for what seemed like years. More than likely, it had something to do with girls. So, I bought them a couple of sodas from the tackle shop in hopes of prying a little information from them or possibly scoring a free casting lesson. Anyone clever enough to keep the fly line in a bucket covered in water so that it didn't dry out exceeded my meager knowledge by light years.

So, for the next hour or two, we stood shoulder to shoulder and watched a large school of snook in the surf stacked shoulder to shoulder watching us. The snook lay up in the trough facing south about sixty feet north of the pier. Dozens of snook were lying there with their noses pointed south into the current. They didn't seem to be interested in anything, much less apt to take a fly. Pilchards were everywhere, and a large school of finger mullet moved up and down the beach. Every once in a while, you would see a big jack crash the pilchards and then beat feet down the beach looking for another easy meal. I'm not sure why the snook weren't feeding; it's possible there was too much bait, which can happen, or perhaps the snook were just full. Perhaps they were getting ready to spawn. The reasons are hard to fathom.

Over the years I have tried hard not to fry too many brain cells trying to understand something that is indecipherable. Years later, I would run into the same situation up and down the beaches on the west coast. Snook can be finicky at times, especially the closer they get to spawning. At best, Brandon could get one to follow his fly every now and then, but he could never get one to take. We stared into the water for what seemed like hours. I didn't get a free casting lesson, but I did learn a lot by watching them and listening to them talk about flies, leaders, and something called a sink tip; then again, it might have been a shooting head. From what I gathered, there seemed to be little difference between the two. After all, what did I know? I was the proud owner of an incinerated fly rod and two ugly flies—not exactly Lefty Kreh.

Thinking back, it's incredible how much of our life was spent standing on a pier, a bridge, or a beach just staring into the abyss, either looking for fish or just watching the tide run by. We didn't think much about it when we were young, but our life was measured by the rise and fall of the tides. Later in life you start to count the number of tide changes you have left, and then you come to the harsh realization that someday it will all end. Then you sense an air of inevitability hovering over everything you do. When we were young, life was incredibly simple. We fished, we surfed, we went to school, and more often than not, we just screwed around and had fun at the pier. It wasn't complicated, but sooner or later you start to wonder when it will all change. We had already seen it happen to some of the older kids.

Too many ended up in Vietnam and never came back, and the ones who did come back were never quite the same. They were different in ways we could never understand. Over the years, life began to entail much more than just fishing or surfing—it's who we were and, for the most part, still are. Of course, at that time I might not have been able to express myself as well as I can now—after all, I was still in the eighth grade.

The ocean has always had a great allure; it's almost mesmerizing. I think it's because you only glean a sliver of the abyss at any one time. As the years go by, you stop thinking of yourself as just a fisherman or just a surfer. You start to look at things through the eyes of a waterman. Waterman is a surfing term typically not associated with fishing for some reason, but it should be. Not a landlubber, but a waterman, someone who spends his life on the water or in the water. It's a small distinction most people couldn't care less about, but at some point you need to define who you are.

Looking back, it seems like we were always grasping at some sort of legitimacy or belonging. It's as if we needed to be better than the kids who came from good homes and attentive parents—even though we would have never traded our world for theirs. Life can be complicated at times. Relationships with other kids at school tended toward the downright frustrating. I am not sure anyone ever understood us. It was a little easier on me than others because I played football and baseball, and thus in some ways I had a foot in both worlds.

• *10* •

The One and Only Splendid Splinter

*S*everal months after my second less-than-fruitful introduction to fly fishing, I was in Sears, Roebuck checking out the tackle section. In the fly-fishing section, and I use that term gingerly, I found a Ted Williams seven foot nine saltwater fly rod with a Shakespeare fly reel on sale. I want to say it only cost me thirty-five or forty dollars. It couldn't have cost much more. In any event, it cost more than I had on hand. In fact, I had to sell a Penn 710 spinning reel on a Gator Glass rod to buy the fly rod. But it put me back in business—in a way. I had a new fly rod, but I still didn't have any backing or a fly line, much less know how to tie the complicated saltwater leaders everyone kept telling me about. All I had for flies were the two ugly creations I had tied at the fly-club meeting in Travis's garage. Still, I was on a roll.

Feelings of the ignorant can be misleading. Turns out that learning to fly-fish is not something one should attempt on one's own. It's not that it's too complicated, but it can be at times. It's like the Everglades when you're learning your way around: it's best to start at the corners; that way you don't get lost.

Unlike today, formal instruction wasn't easy to come by. I think the only reason Sears carried fly rods was because of Ted Williams. I remember watching him demonstrating how to cast at the Bahia Mar Marina at the annual Fort Lauderdale Boat Show. The crowd was so large I couldn't get within a hundred feet of the casting pool, if there was such a thing. For all I know, Ted could have been standing on a piece of carpet. Like I said, the crowd was enormous. I don't remember if I wanted to see him cast, or I just wanted to see Ted Williams, the all-time greatest hitter in baseball—the one and only Splendid Splinter, The Kid, Teddy Ballgame, The Thumper, whatever you want to call him. He was the man. At least that's what my father always told me.

41

As the years went by, Ted Williams became one of the world's best-known fly fishermen. It didn't matter if he had a bat in his hand or a fly rod, or if he was in the cockpit of a Grumman F9F Panther he flew in combat—Ted exemplified Ernest Hemingway's famous definition of style: "grace under pressure."

Ted excelled in almost anything and everything he wanted to do, except maybe marriage and parenting. In the immortal words of Leonard McCoy, aka Bones, to Spock in *The Voyage Home*, "No one is perfect."

Until this time, the only fly rod I had attempted to cast was the pathetic hand-me-down fly rod, which had been handed down too many times. That experiment had only lasted two or three days before I ended its miserable existence. Having failed to get meaningful instruction from Ted Williams, I desperately needed someone who knew how to rig my new fly rod. So, I called Brandon.

Later that evening, he showed up at the pier with a spool of backing, a new fly line, leader material, and thirty flies or so. Most of the flies were tied for the salt, but he did bring a small assortment of bass bugs. Brandon taught me how to rig the fly rod. Next, he set about teaching me how to tie a Bimini twist and something called a nail knot so I could attach the tapered leader to the fly line. He explained the dynamics of a tapered leader and the relationship of the butt section to the remaining six feet of the leader. Leaders can be a touchy topic at times. Everyone seems to have an opinion, and that's fine as long as I don't have to be part of the conversation. Over time, I learned to stay out of the useless pissing matches about lines, leaders, and knots, and especially, flies.

Back in the day, fly fishing was still relatively simple, at least it could be—only a handful of companies specialized in saltwater fly-fishing, so you wouldn't think there would be much to argue about. It's almost as bad as arguing about sports with someone who never watches sports; or even worse, someone who never played the game.

Often it pays just to shut up and learn. Brandon spent the next several months teaching me everything he knew about fly-fishing. His dad, Ralph, was a well-known guide, and although Brandon was still relatively young, he was an up-and-coming superstar. We spent two, sometimes three hours a day after school on the high-school football field just casting. I invested days and days learning how to double haul. Looking back, that could have been the greatest value-added benefit bestowed on my life—besides my wife and family. You have to remember that we were still using glass rods back in the early seventies. You had to slow to a crawl to get the rod to load.

Fast-forward, and modern-day fly rods are made from space-age graphite and tend to be so fast that essentially anyone can pick one up and in a day or two be throwing forty or fifty feet of line. For those of us who grew up with glass rods, and in some cases, bamboo fly rods, the new graphite rods are almost sacrilegious—that is, unless you happen to be throwing an overweighted permit fly the size of a silver dollar seventy feet into a thirty-mile-an-hour gale.

That being said, in some cases, modern-day graphite sticks do serve a purpose. What's life without a little hypocrisy now and then? Heck, I find it tough to make it through the day without at least one juicy rationalization. Great minds might argue a cerebral side to all this back-and-forth about leaders, lines, backing, and materials—specific components required to make a great fly rod. My feeble mind maintains that a great caster is precisely that: a great caster. Anything else is just a waste of breath—like arguing about politics and religion. Then again, we talk about what we love (or what we deem ourselves experts in). Fly fishermen pontificate about anything and everything that has to do with fly-fishing, especially gear.

Nor is our tribe immune to cliquishness: you have three types of fishermen—fly fishermen, conventional fishermen, and pragmatists. Fly fishermen usually don't mix with traditional fishermen, and conventional fishermen normally can't stand fly fishermen. The former consider the other tribe vulgar rednecks; the latter know deep in their hearts that every single member of the former tribe is guilty of pseudo-intellectual snobbery to the highest degree. Pragmatists live in both worlds and see the fly rod as just another club in the bag. If the situation is right, take out the fly rod; if it's windy and hard to cast, go for a spinning or baitcasting rod—whatever gets the job done and keeps you on the water. In the beginning, when fly-fishing was new to our shores, pragmatism ruled. Fishing was fishing, and although fly-fishing was a hoot, it certainly wasn't the only or best way to catch a fish. Something tells me I just blew my movie deal.

Fort Liquordale, in All Its Glory

*E*ven though I was starting to get the hang of pitching a fly, I still hadn't made a cast at a living target. But things were about to change for the better. After fishing the outgoing tide at Anglin's Pier without much to show for our time, Brandon, Ron, and I decided to head down to the local Denny's on the corner of I-95 and Commercial Boulevard to have breakfast while we waited for the tide to change. Any restaurant in Fort Liquordale near I-95 after midnight rivaled a night at the *Rocky Horror Picture Show*. You could run into just about anybody: from the down-and-out to the filthy rich rolling out of new Ferraris, to a limousine full of strippers from the nearby men's clubs that once lined I-95 from Pompano Beach to Hollywood.

Restrooms constituted an adventure in themselves. More often than not, the bathrooms were full of junkies shooting up, selling drugs, or panhandling. The waitresses seemed to go with the flow and didn't bat an eye if a couple decided to have sex in one of the booths—as long as they tipped well. Telling who was who, what was what, and which pronoun to use to describe specific individuals among the clientele had its challenges.

Fort Liquordale, in all its glory and all its transgressions, was always entertaining and, at the same time, a little disgusting. But, because we had grown up in Fort Liquordale, we considered it almost run-of-the-mill. I am not sure what it would have taken to shock us. Anyway, all I wanted was a large stack of pancakes with bacon and a fresh cup of coffee.

After breakfast, Brandon's dad, Ralph, met us at the Seventeenth Street causeway boat ramp, though it could have been the Fifteenth Street causeway boat ramp. We planned to fish the lights around the local docks and then hit the fender lights around the bridges when the tide started to ebb. This momentous night combined two firsts for me: first time fishing out of a flats boat and first time pitching a fly anywhere near a real fish.

We pulled up to the boat ramp, and Ralph already had the boat in the water with the engine running. We were starting to load our gear when Ralph grabbed my new fly rod and held it up to the lights on the dock for a few seconds, then told me to take it back to the truck. Ralph told me not to worry: he had several fly rods in the boat already rigged. At least he didn't say get that piece of crap out of my boat. I was free to convince myself that we were looking more at a logistical issue than at quality control.

Fully equipped, we idled out of the boat basin until we turned the corner. Then, Ralph jumped on it, and, in a matter of seconds, we screamed down the Intracoastal Waterway headed to Port Everglades to fish some-place called the "hot water canal." Flats boats are made to run in extremely skinny water; if they are trimmed right, that leaves very little of the hull in the water, especially with a lot of horsepower to waste. More often than not, it can make for a squirrelly ride. Fortunately, we had a calm night, a full moon, and strong tides. A few thunderstorms had pushed through early in the evening; at that moment, the sky was clear.

That day I experienced Port Everglades up close for the first time. Port Everglades is an incredibly busy port. At times, even the navy has a few smaller ships tied off there. I had seen it countless times before from the bridge and from the beaches. But for some reason, it looked substantially larger from the vantage point of a sixteen-foot flats boat. The port itself is primarily an industrial waterway, but it's surrounded on all sides by multimillion-dollar mansions that stay vacant nine months of the year. The majority of these million-dollar neighborhoods had great canals, and almost every waterfront home came equipped with a dock adorned in wonderful lights.

It didn't take long to reach the hot water canal; for some reason I had anticipated a much longer boat ride. But then, I didn't have any idea where the hot water canal was or what it was. It turned out to be the discharge canal for the Florida Power & Light plant. FP&L sucked the colder seawater into the plant to cool the turbines, then pumped the warmer water back into the port via the hot water canal. We eased into the canal and slowly worked our way through. Because the canal's temperature exceeded the water temperature in the port by several degrees, it formed a veritable fish magnet.

Several other flats boats were drifting down the canal. Ralph knew most of them and stopped to chat with two of them. From what I could tell, they had hooked several midsize tarpon on each float. That was good news, I thought: at least there were fish. The more they talked, the more evident it became that I wouldn't get a shot with the fly rod. The other boats were all using glow-in-the-dark plastic bait—something they called trout touts. They were floating down the canal, bouncing the touts on the bottom. Ralph told me to hang on tight because the tarpon would crush the baits and nearly pull you overboard—especially if you managed to hook one of the mammoth-size tarpon from the Paleozoic that often frequented the canal.

We idled up the canal another half mile or so, and Ralph shut down the engine. We couldn't go any further—fifty-gallon drums were strung across the hot water canal via a massive cable. This was as close as FP&L was going to let us get to the discharge pipes. Brandon and Ron grabbed a couple of bait-casting outfits and started pitching plastic bait as close to the seawall and mangroves as they could get, then bounced them on the bottom as we slowly drifted down the canal. Ralph told me to hang in there, and as soon as one of the boys jumped one, I was up next. It almost sounded fair in a prejudiced sort of way—after all, I was the only rookie in the boat. Then again, Brandon's father did own the flats boat. I did my best to temper my enthusiasm and, at the same time, not show my disappointment.

When we were young, patience is not a virtue we demonstrated very often. It didn't take long before Brandon set the hook on the first tarpon. It jumped four or five times and then spit the hook, which usually happens when you hook a small tarpon with a jig. Young tarpon shake their heads so violently at times that more often than not, they throw the weighted jig head—often at you, especially in close quarters. Ralph told Brandon to sit down and let me try. I thought Brandon was going to push me over the side of the boat for a moment when I slid by him, but he finally capitulated, reeled in, and went back to talk to his father. Like any street-smart kid, I kept my distance. I made my way to the bow, and before I had time to make a cast, Ron hooked a tarpon. Ralph started the engine, turned the boat around, and tried to follow, but by the time he got the boat pointed in the right direction, it was too late. Actually, it was too late the minute Ron hooked the big tarpon.

As far as canals go, the hot water canal was relatively small. Based on my fifteen minutes of experience, we continually had to navigate around other boats. I could only assume that if a spooked fish opted for the other direction, it would swim under the barrels that stretched the width of the canal. The foregone conclusion: we would lose the fish.

By this time the tarpon had emptied Ron's spool, and the line snapped with a loud pop. All Ron could say was, "Damn, that was a big fish," even though I don't think he used the "d" word to describe his excitement. Ralph ran the skiff back up to the barrels that blocked off the canal. This time Brandon was on the bow, and I was fishing a little farther back on the starboard side. But instead of casting toward the seawall, I was casting down current and picking up the line as we drifted back down the canal. I was doing essentially the same thing they were, but I was fishing the deeper water; this way, my trout tout was always close to the bottom. Of course, you always had to be aware of all the slack line. It had been my experience that most fish crush the jig on the drop, not the upswing, regardless of the species. It has something to do with the slack line. I think that when the jig is floating back to the bottom, it looks more natural, because the line has no tension on it.

We had drifted about five or six hundred yards when I saw a massive boil about thirty feet off the starboard bow. I reeled in my line as fast as I could and pitched the plastic bait directly over Brandon's head. When the bait landed, my line settled down over Brandon's left shoulder. He looked back and said, "Are you kidding me? I can't believe you did that."

I don't think I responded. I just lifted up the rod tip and the line over Brandon's head and accidentally knocked his hat into the water. Ralph almost fell off the poling platform, laughing. Evidently, an unwritten protocol pertains to a flats boat: its first rule is never cast over the head of the guy on the bow of the boat.

Unhindered by such regulations through my youthful (or useful) ignorance, I started reeling in my plastic bait. The tout hung down in the water a foot or so beneath the surface. While I was enjoying spirited instruction on boat etiquette from Brandon, a tremendous boil right beneath the port gunwale grabbed my attention. It hit my bait so hard I almost lost the rod. Startled, I set the hook as hard as I could under the circumstances. It was a miracle that the line didn't break. Line started screaming off my reel at warp speed, but the fish never jumped. Ralph did. He started the engine, and we were off to the races, or so we thought. The fish wasn't headed down the canal; it swam straight to the mangroves, and there was little I could do about it. I put my thumb on the spool to slow it down; it helped a little but not as much as I had hoped. What it did accomplish was burning my thumb; you could smell it. And, yes, if you are wondering, it hurt like heck.

The fish started to come to the surface. Ralph pulled out his spotlight and turned it on. When he pointed the light at the fish, I almost fell out of the boat. Here we were face to tail with a thirty-pound snook, give or take a few pounds. Ron kept screaming, "Look at his line—look at his line."

The first thirty feet of my line were frayed to shreds. If my snook reached the mangroves, I could do nothing to stop him. Ralph picked up the push pole and tried his best to keep us out of the mangroves. I kept pumping the rod and reeling on the down stroke. It got to the point that every time I pumped the rod, instead of moving the snook, more line peeled off the reel.

For the most part, it wasn't much different than trying to keep a big snook out of the pilings at the pier. Ralph, always the consummate guide, kept screaming out directions—but, to be honest, I wasn't listening. Of course, this was the first time Ralph and I had ever fished together, and he probably didn't know what to expect from me. In any event, the snook and I were engaged in a relentless tug of war. I was doing everything I could to keep him from the mangroves. I tried hard not to think about losing the snook. In the end, it's normally a self-fulfilling prophecy. The longer the fight lasts, the smaller the chance you have of landing the fish. The primary concern on my mind was the frayed line. It held. After another ten minutes or so, the fish was beside the boat. Ralph grabbed the snook by the tail and tried to lift it into the boat. Brandon yelled, "It's got to be a MET fish."

"Okay, I will bite. What the hell is a MET fish?" I asked. All three of them looked at me like I was a blithering idiot. But none of them took the time to explain what a MET fish really was. I knew what the snook was—it was mine. Instead, Ron had already started filling the live well. Ralph lifted the fish into the live well. All he could do was smile and give me a high five. In reality, I should have been giving him the high five; if it hadn't been for his quick thinking and boatmanship, I would never have landed the snook.

Brandon, being Brandon, looked back at me and started reading me the riot act again. Sometimes you can't win. I can only assume that Brandon thought the fish should have been his. What I didn't understand was how the line got so frayed in the first place and why it didn't break. A snook has razor-sharp gill plates, and when you catch one, the leader is almost always frayed. This time the line was frayed twenty or thirty feet from the leader. The only thing that could have happened is that the snook ran around or under something when it hit the trout tout. No telling what or who lies at the bottom of the hot water canal.

Strip, Strip, as Fast as You Can

$\mathcal{D}$ays later, I found out what had caused the line to fray. One of the ceramic guides was cracked just enough to pinch the line when the snook took off. The cracked guide shredded the light line. Incredibly, the line never snapped, although it should never have happened in the first place. All I had to do was run a short piece of my mother's stockings through the guides. The stockings would have gotten stuck in the crack, and I could have replaced it. From top to bottom, the job would have taken me thirty minutes. Then all I had to do was paint the color preserver on the thread, layer several coats of epoxy on the new wrapping, and let it dry.

Up to this point, I had never heard of the MET (Miami Metropolitan Fishing Tournament). Throughout the night and later that morning at breakfast at the Floridian on Las Olas Boulevard, I learned more about the MET than any kid who couldn't afford to fish the MET should know. The truth is that I could fish the MET, but I couldn't afford to compete in the MET. The glory days of the MET had come and gone for kids like me. At one time, it was almost exclusively a guide's tournament, and for the most part, only people with money and the free time participated in the MET. By the time I came along, I was too young, and the MET was too old, and my parents weren't wealthy enough.

We floated the hot water canal several more times without much fanfare. Finally, Ralph decided it was time to hit the lights at Pier 66. So, we idled into the mouth of the marina and started checking out the lights. Not only did the docks have lights, but the majority of the big battlewagons had tuna towers with lights pointed at the water. On the other hand, the tide was blowing out, Ralph really didn't want to anchor in the small channel, and it didn't look like the security guards would let us tie off on the docks. On the upside, bait was everywhere. We saw snook and tarpon stacked up under most of the lights.

Even where we couldn't see snook or tarpon, we knew they were there. Every few minutes we heard a loud pop under the lights: big snook sucking down pilchards or taking a big shrimp off the surface. The place was alive. We could feel the electricity in the air. All we had to do was figure out a way to fish the lights without spooking any fish. The best way to fish would have been from the docks and not the skiff. The odds are, if you manage to hook a big snook or a tarpon anywhere around the lights, the fish wraps your line around the closest piling and cuts you off with the speed and accuracy of a straight razor.

Ralph decided to run up current and try to put the skiff in the right position to float close enough but not so close that it would spook the fish. He decided that it was time to break out the fly rods. I thought this would be a great time to take the high road and surrender the bow to Brandon or Ron. I couldn't help anticipating that my initial efforts at casting contained potential for embarrassment.

Brandon jumped up on the bow first and started stripping line off the reel like he had done this a thousand times before, and he probably had. I, on the other hand, had never even stood this close to someone who knew what he was doing, much less from the bow of a flats skiff. Brandon didn't bother with long, lazy casts; he pounded the line under the docks like a pile driver. His body was contorted in multiple positions at the same time, and the odd thing about it was, he looked relaxed doing it. I knew from the start that I was entirely out of my league. I was playing pewee baseball, and they were chasing the National League pennant.

At least he didn't hook up on every cast. Even though he had a ridiculous number of snook and tarpon follow his fly, none took it. He started to get pissed. I didn't blame him; I was getting frustrated myself, and I was in the back of the boat. Ron seemed extremely flustered, waiting for his turn. He kept walking up and down the small boat. Ralph finally had to tell him to sit down. He was making everyone in the boat nervous. At this point I was about ready to jump off the boat and swim home. I kept thinking all I needed was a big, fat handpicked shrimp. Fly-fishing can be a paradox at times: we could have caught dozens of snook and tarpon that night using live bait, but we stood there watching Brandon make cast after cast without hooking up once.

We floated the docks several more times. Brandon and Ron beat the water into froth repeatedly. Finally, the tide slowed, and the sun inched its way over the horizon. The result was a mixture of early morning thunderstorm and an incredibly brilliant sunrise. Only in the tropics and subtropics does this happen: you can feel the static electricity of the thunderstorm in its intensity all the way down to your bones, followed by the early morning heat of the sun.

You duck from lightning strikes too far in the distance to matter and startle from thunder so loud you can almost see the water ripple.

Early morning has always been my favorite time of the day to be on the water. As we cleared the corner, just barely missing the bow of one of the massive sport fishermen, the water erupted everywhere around our skiff. The effect was as variously explosive as lighting a match to a Coleman lantern with the fuel valve wide open. Monster jack crevalle the size of small Volkswagens busted bait everywhere around us. There had to be hundreds of them, causing the water to turn various shades of blue and yellow—mixed with the thick white froth and foam created by the feeding frenzy. Ralph grabbed a fly rod and changed the fly almost instantly. You have to love fishing with an experienced guide, especially on his day off.

Then Ralph handed me the fly rod. I didn't have time to think. I started stripping line off the reel, and when I had thirty or forty feet of fly line lying on the deck, I began to cast. Of course, I had the line stacked in reverse, and on my first cast the fly line ended up in a bird's nest. I waited somewhat bashfully (and impatiently) for Brandon and Ron to untangle my line for me so I could make another cast. I harbored a suspicion that it would take years to live down that brilliant first cast.

Once my line could be returned to active duty, I started casting and double hauling. This time, my fly landed in the middle of the bait. Ralph screamed, "Strip, strip, strip, as fast as you can!"

So, I started stripping as fast as I could. On every third strip, the fly line slipped out of my hand, requiring me to start all over. I was getting frustrated. The more frustrated I got, the worse my casting became. In the end, I couldn't even find the pathetic approximation of the stroke that I had mustered on dry land.

"Take a deep breath, slow down, and relax," Ralph instructed me.

I did. On the last strip, before I picked up my line off the water to make another cast, an enormous jack came out from under the boat and slammed my fly.

By this time the jack was a hundred yards into the backing. It dawned on me that if I didn't stop the fish, or at least slow it down, it would end up with a front-row seat at the next Jimmy Buffett concert at the Bayside Marina, enjoying a rum runner and a laugh at my expense.

Ralph started up the engine, pointed the skiff south, and slowly started following the big jack. If he went too fast, the boat would overrun the fly line, and the fish would probably spit the hook. If he went too slowly, I would lose more line off the reel. The problem was that I really didn't know how to fight a big fish with a fly rod. After all, this was the only fish I had ever hooked on a fly rod. I was getting on-the-job training in real time.

In some ways, it was like any other kind of fishing. You could only exert so much pressure on the line at any given time. The closer you are to the fish, the more pressure you can exert, and the faster you can tire out the fish. Of course, everything comes at a price: if you put too much pressure on the fish, the hook could pull out, the tippet could break, and any number of things can prevent you from landing the fish. In the end, the last thing you want to do is to bring a green fish to the boat. It might make sense for the fish's sake to bring him to the boat green. The jack expends less energy and probably has a better chance of survival, but I have seen too many fish go the other way.

Forty-five minutes later, Ralph grabbed the jack by the tail. It took everything he could do to calm the fish. The jack was still comparatively green, and it was in the process of beating itself senseless on the side of the boat. Ralph lifted the massive jack over the gunwales; Brandon took out the fly; Ron snapped a few Polaroids; the adventure was over. Before anyone could say anything, I slipped the jack back over the gunwales, gave it a few back and forth by the tail, and then watched the enormous jack slowly swim away. I didn't catch as much grief for that as I had expected. To my mind, Brandon and Ron went back to the stern of the skiff and sat down on the lid of the live wells a bit wistfully, as if to say to themselves: *It will never happen; stop thinking about it.*

Although looking back, I wish I had also released the snook I had caught earlier. Little did I know, it was probably a female, and she would have laid tens of thousands of eggs throughout her lifetime. We ran back up to Pier 66, and by the time we got there, the sun was breaking on the water, and the tide had slowed to a snail's pace.

An hour from now, the tide would be ripping, but for the next half hour or so, the tide would be at peace with itself. The glaring sun would drive most of the fish deeper into the dark shadows of the abyss until it was time to feed again. Most would move off and sulk until the tide started to rip. Fish that take up residence in and around marinas, piers, and pilings rarely change locations, but they do change directions, and they seem to keep their noses pointed into the current. The magic hour for most saltwater game fish is a half hour before sunrise and the first half hour after sunrise—similar to the magic hour around midnight, which, according to *Midnight in the Garden of Good and Evil*, is apparently bifurcated into a half hour for doing good and a half hour for doing evil: "Boy, if you want to understand the living you have to commune with the dead."

In a roundabout way, that pretty much summarizes late-night or, rather, early-morning, tides: a half hour before sunrise to catch fish and a half hour after sunrise to do mischief. If the voodoo priestess Minerva had been a fisherman, she probably would have augmented her elucidation to, "Boy, if you want to learn how to catch fish, then you have to commune with the guide."

Minerva was the wife of the famous voodoo priest Dr. Buzzard.

We pulled the boat and headed to the Floridian for breakfast to round out our late-night excursion. Over a large stack of pancakes, bacon, and countless cups of coffee, I received an education on the MET and various other faux pas I had committed on the boat that night. My cohorts also showered me with a good dose of "good-natured" ribbing for my bumbling the first cast and unfathomable beginner's luck. Once Brandon and the others were satisfied that I understood the unwritten rules of boat etiquette and the history of the MET, we left the Floridian. We pulled out onto Los Olas Boulevard, and several hundred yards down the road we took a right turn into the parking lot of the local tackle shop. Ralph had barely stopped the truck when Brandon and Ron bounded into the shop.

Looking back, I probably should have just stayed in the truck. Little did I know at the time that my life was about to change. I was about to enter the world of some of the most obsessed and insane fishermen on the planet.

• *13* •

It Was All about Competition

*H*ave you ever done something that you intuitively knew was wrong, and the little voice in your head kept telling you to "run for the stronghold Thunderheart—run for the stronghold."

Have you ever turned right when you should have turned left? Maybe you took the road most traveled when you should have taken the road less traveled? Someone somewhere should have told me to listen to my inner voice. I was about to get involved with some of the most enthusiastic drug addicts on the planet. Only their drug of choice wasn't heroin or some other illicit hallucinogenic. It was nothing more than old-fashioned competition. Don't get me wrong: competition can be healthy at times. It's what makes the world go round. Someone asked Ted Williams once what he thought of fishing tournaments, and he replied, "I object to fishing tournaments less for what they do to fish than what they do to the fisherman."

This is odd because Ted Williams was one of the most competitive people on the planet. But I do understand the distinction between a great baseball player chasing pennants and the slaughtering of gamefish to see your name up in lights.

Fishermen are competitive by nature. No one wants to be outfished by anyone, much less his fishing buddies. This was different; this was nothing more than an excuse for fishermen to stroke their own egos. They wanted to see their names in the newspaper. Every Sunday, the *Miami Herald* posted the results of the largest fish caught and weighed in each division for the previous week in the sports section. Fishermen wanted to see their names on the plaques and trophies that would eventually adorn the walls of their office or tackle shop. I didn't know it at the time, but I would eventually grow to hate fishing tournaments, and I'm sad to say, I wasn't a big fan of the fishermen who participated in them either.

The companies that sponsored the tournaments used the MET as nothing more than a walking, talking infomercial. The MET was used to peddle its latest toys and make money on the death of thousands, if not tens of thousands, of gamefish over the years. Up to this point, I had always thought fishing and surfing were more about a philosophical approach to nature and not competition. I never thought about fishing or surfing as a sport, even though I love sports. I was the world's biggest Miami Dolphins fan on the planet. The words sports and fishing should never have been used in the same sentence.

Sometimes I think competition is so hardwired in our DNA that we don't even notice it. I remember sitting on my grandfather's lap in the front of an old worn-out johnboat on one of the tributaries of Lake Eufaula in Alabama banging plastic worms off old cypress trunks and high clay banks for bass. I must have been around four or five years old at the time. My uncle was in the back of the boat running the trolling motor and pitching black or blue rubber worms with a Zebco Spincast 33.

He was convinced that black or blue rubber worms, a few split shot, and a bag or two of weedless hooks were the only things you needed in your tackle box. The banter between my grandfather and my uncle Robert was never ending. They started yapping at each other from the minute they pushed the boat away from the bank. One morning we hadn't even made it around the first bend when my uncle hooked a largemouth bass at the mouth of a muddy creek that flowed in and around two massive old-growth pine trees that had washed away when the muddy bank collapsed. The bass had to be pushing nine or ten pounds. It almost destroyed his Zebco. The poor reel never worked right again, and you can guess which reel my uncle gave me to fish with the next time we went fishing.

Looking back, I don't have any idea how long it took him to get the bass close enough to the net, but from my vantage point, it seemed like hours. Of course, you have to remember, I was only four or five years old at the time, and minutes probably seemed like hours. Then again, he was using a Zebco 33.

The entire time my uncle was fighting the enormous bass, my grandfather never looked back. He wouldn't even acknowledge the fact that my uncle had a fish on. My uncle asked him to help net the fish, and my grandfather wouldn't lift a finger to save his life. In the end, my uncle netted the fish and put it in the cooler. When he finally made it back to the trailer/cabin, he wrapped the bass in plastic wrap, even though I think they called it cellophane wrap in those days, but I could be wrong. My uncle put the bass in the freezer.

When anyone would come over for dinner, my uncle Robert would drag the old bass out of the fridge and show it off. My uncle and my grandfather were so competitive and jealous of each other that they rarely, if ever, talked about the fish. It was as if the behemoth largemouth never existed. It wasn't until years later that I understood what was happening between my grandfather and my uncle.

I understood what competition was all about long before the first day I showed up at the pier, so at least I had some half-assed idea of what to expect. Of course, I really didn't care what people thought or what they had to say. The only chance you had to impress the tribe was to prove to everyone you knew what you were doing. Then again, a little flattery never hurt. The kids at the pier could be incredibly tribalistic at times and extremely cruel when they wanted to be. At some point, you had to bark the other kids down, then prove to them that you had what it takes to challenge the alpha male of the group. Not everyone was made to thrive in that type of situation, and not everyone did. In some ways, competition defines the parameters of the situation. It either sets you apart from the tribe or it defines your position in the tribe.

At Anglin's Pier, it was all about competition. Of course, it was always your decision whether you wanted to participate. As awful as this sounds, it's child's play compared to a surfing lineup. But that's another story altogether. As a Jamaican friend of mine once said, "Life on the streets can be hard, man."

Marcus Aurelius once wrote, "It's simple, stop caring what other people think. Stop caring what they do. Stop caring what they say. All that matters is what you do. Everything else is beyond your concern. You can let it all go. You can ignore it entirely."

Marcus Aurelius was right, of course, but unfortunately, as much sense as this makes, it's a complicated philosophy to understand much less follow when you're fourteen or fifteen years old. Philosophy was never written for teenagers. Life at the pier was about relationships, peer pressure, and the need to fit in, nothing else.

• *14* •

Don't Forget to Tip the Guide

$\mathcal{R}$alph climbed out of the truck, stepped up on the galvanized mudguards that ran parallel to the trailer, and hopped into the flats boat. If I had tried that with my flip-flops on, I would have slipped and landed on my derriere. Ralph was headed for the Coleman cooler strapped down to the center console. He grunted, lifted up the heavy cooler and laid it down on the starboard gunwale. I pulled the drain plug, and for the next several minutes, we watched two or three gallons of melted ice painstakingly dribble out onto the parking lot.

It seemed a little funny to both of us that Brandon and Ron scrambled into the tackle shop quickly to avoid the heavy lifting. We both grabbed a handle and worked our way to the door. I would like to think that the cooler was heavy because my snook weighed so much, but in reality, the cooler was full of ice, a few beers, and who knows what else. Eventually, fishing coolers have a life of their own. They're passed down from father to son, son to a friend, friend to friend until the cooler falls apart or, in some cases, until someone else absconds with it out of the back of your pickup truck. Years later, when I was attending Florida State University, it was an accepted prank to help oneself to a cooler out of someone else's truck. Even worse, you were expected to keep a six-pack or two inside the cooler so the poor loathsome soul wouldn't die of thirst.

We made it to the front door, and one of the kids working in the shop squeezed through the door and tried to hold it open. Of course, the kid was as wide as the door and, for the most part, didn't grasp the situation. I was waiting for Ralph to chime in with a couple of colorful metaphors; after all, it's a well-known scientific fact that three people and one oversized cooler cannot go through the same door at the same time. But it never stopped anyone from trying. Fishermen, if nothing else, are stubborn to a fault. Finally, we put the cooler on the ground and slid it through the door.

From an early age, virtually anyone who knew me thought I would end up as a guide somewhere in the Florida Keys. Truth be told, from an early age I knew I didn't want to be a guide. I wanted to be the guy on the bow pitching bait at giant chrome-plated tarpon from the Paleozoic, bonefish made of polished silver, or live crabs at permit so large it staggered the imagination.

Until that night, I never knew it would be so complicated. After spending a night on the water with Ralph, I could only assume that guides did this kind of heavy lifting every day. From the look of Ralph's shoulders and his massive forearms, his gnarly sunburned fingers, he had been doing this for quite a while. From what I could tell, the boat was in immaculate shape, everything was in its place, and even better yet, everything had a place. I think Ralph and I shared a common bond. We were both neat freaks.

On the other hand, Brandon, Ralph's one and only offspring, was ridiculously skinny, even to the point of looking anorexic; his shoulders were almost nonexistent. It was hard to believe that Brandon was Ralph's son. From the look of Brandon's bony forearms, Ralph got stuck with most of the heavy lifting, loading and unloading the boat, poling the boat, cleaning the boat, and for the most part, paying for all the gas for both the boat and truck. I'm still not sure what Brandon's responsibility was or if he even had any. Brandon looked more like a surf bum or pier rat than someone who had to work for a living.

Brandon and Ron lived in surf shorts, T-shirts, flip-flops, and Miami Dolphins baseball caps. They had bleached-blond hair and tans that were so dark, they almost seemed painful. Ron was virtually a carbon copy except for the short hair and beard that was nothing more than a few unruly hairs. Of course, I'm not sure I looked any different—then again, I'm not sure any of us looked different.

When Ralph and I finally made it through the door, everyone inside had already heard the whole story. Brandon didn't seem irritated. He just wanted everyone to know that the snook should have been his. In the end, he took the high road, sort of, and for the most part, stopped razzing me in front of the five or six people standing around in the shop. I was surprised that Brandon and Ron didn't recount my exploits on the bow with the fly line. It wasn't that I was shy, but from what I could see, I was the youngest person in the shop, and I had no intention of making a fool of myself.

In the middle of all the conversations, I noticed that Brandon and Ron never mentioned that I was the only one on the boat who caught a fish that night; if I do say so myself, I caught two. I wanted to say so many things that morning but didn't, and yes, discretion is the better part of valor some-times, especially when you're young and sometimes a tad arrogant.

Ralph heaved the cooler up on top of a chest freezer in the back room. One or two people made a few off-the-cuff remarks about the size of the snook, but it was a nice fish even though I had seen much larger snook at the pier. I had lost a lot of snook at Anglin's Pier that would have dwarfed the one lying on the chest freezer. One of the kids lifted the snook out of the cooler and flopped it down on what looked like an old-fashioned produce scale hanging from the rafters, the kind you might see at the farmers' markets that once lined the rural roads of Homestead and Davie. It was the first time I remember feeling uneasy about killing a snook.

By this time, the snook had lost most of its muscular shape. The iridescent colors on the fins had lost their luster as if someone had turned off the light switch. The black lateral line that once glowed in the dark had faded the way a silver plate oxidizes and then tarnishes. It was nothing more than a lifeless, washed-out slab of fish lying on the scale. It didn't seem like much to brag about, much less get your name in the newspaper for killing something so beautiful. The scale bounced up and down, the arm on the scale went back and forth, and when the bouncing finally stopped, it settled at a few ounces over twenty-eight pounds. That wasn't surprising, considering that it had been on ice for several hours. Fish frequently lose two, sometimes three pounds if you don't weigh them right away.

The owner of the shop handed me a folder that contained all the rules and regulations for the MET. I remember thinking this is ridiculous. It reminded me of homework. In the end, that was precisely what it was, a lot of work, reading anything and everything I could find, endless hours at the library, as if I had time to waste. I put most of the information in a folder except for the information card I had to fill out. In the process of filling out the card, I had to describe the type of rod and reel and the pound test line I was using. I was lucky this time; I had used Ralph's rod even though mine was lashed down under the gunwale. Just dumb luck. Ralph's rod was built to conform to the MET specifications. Suddenly it dawned on me that I didn't own one rod that would meet the specifications of the MET except for my one and only Ted Williams fly rod. I had to ponder the question—what would it take to fish the tournament and win? I would have to give up my free time, rebuild my rods, and spend what little money I had, as if I had any to waste.

Then I had to find transportation and explain all of this to my parents, if they even cared. In the end, what would I get out of this? If I had had any brains at the time, I would have taken my snook, walked out of the tackle shop, and waited in the truck for Ralph and the boys. Life was getting complicated. I was spinning in too many different directions at the same time and going nowhere, like a cat high on catnip chasing its tail but never catching it.

I didn't know it at the time, but my world was about to spin into an empty universe. To make things even worse, I was about to lose control of my fairy-tale life, the life I loved and fought desperately to keep.

The next day I began to explain my predicament to my mother. Looking around, I asked her where my stepfather, John, was. I thought he should be in on the conversation because the money was going to come out of his pocket. She seemed hesitant to tell me, but after a few minutes of playing twenty questions, she finally gave in. Through a far-reaching acquaintance, my stepfather knew someone who knew someone who was looking for a willing partner who knew something about the hotel and restaurant business to help him open a seafood restaurant on Siesta Key. As I picked myself up off the floor, I politely asked my mother, "Where in the hell is Siesta Key?" After a few more colorful metaphors, she asked me if I was through using all the filthy language. She said it was in Sarasota. She and my stepfather had talked it over, and they thought I would love it there.

My next question was, when? I knew that we were just renting. We always rented, and it was nothing for them to pick up and move at a moment's notice. The timing was perfect for my parents. It was Christmas break. I had plenty of time to help pack.

When you are young, moving is a miserable experience unless you really want to get away from the present situation, which I most certainly did not. I bolted from the house, jumped on my bike, and made my way to the pier. I think I told the same story fifty times over the next several days. I had no intention of moving to Sarasota, but at some point, you realize you don't have any control over your life.

Long-Haired Hippies, Surfboards, and Wet Suits

$\mathcal{U}$nfortunately for me, my stepfather managed to buy into the restaurant. I was so angry I don't remember much about the move. I helped my parents pack, but I asked Brandon and Ron to help me pack my fishing gear and six or seven of my best surfboards, then follow my parents' moving van across the Alley, then north to Sarasota. In the end, Ralph offered to help, which was a good thing because I needed two pickups. I think Ralph just wanted to see Boca Grande Pass, Charlotte Harbor, and a place he called Englewood. Even though Ralph had never fished the west coast, he was exponentially more interested in the area than I was.

Leaving was difficult. I had to leave my friends, I had to leave my school again, and I had to leave the world I grew up in. In reality, Sarasota was only about four hours down the road, but for someone who wasn't old enough to drive, Fort Lauderdale might as well have been on the other side of the planet. On the other hand, I had been to Sarasota several times; it was a clean city, and compared to Fort Lauderdale, it was relatively small. What I remembered most about my previous trips was all the empty space between Naples and Sarasota, and a fishing pier was about a half hour south of Sarasota.

My parents had found a house on Siesta Key to rent, of course. It wasn't much to brag about, but then again, if it was like all the other homes we lived in, we probably wouldn't be there very long. My stepfather was now part owner of a new restaurant at the end of Midnight Pass Road. They named it, of all things, Happy Land Seafood Restaurant—why, I had no idea. I was almost embarrassed to tell anyone about the restaurant, and even worse, that my stepfather was part owner of something that started with the name Happy Land.

The house might have been on the smaller side, but the lot was huge. The landscaping was beautiful. The front yard was covered with sable palms of all shapes and sizes in a multitude of lime greens and various shades of burnt sienna. The back fence, if you could call it that, was a variation of saw palmetto and several other plants I couldn't name at the time. We had several key lime trees and a giant mango tree; and in the backyard, an enormous gumbo limbo tree shaded the entire back side of the house. If I hadn't thought my parents would have killed me, or worse, the owner would have thrown us out on our rear ends, I would have built a wonderful tree house in that old gumbo limbo and probably lived in it like the Swiss Family Robinson. Imagine being shipwrecked, adrift from my parent's influence, with the freedom to do anything I wanted to and still live in the backyard and close enough to the refrigerator to avoid starving to death.

The first thing my parents did was build one of those tacky above-ground swimming pools you find at Sears—the ones that always had pink flamingos and make-believe palm trees painted on the side. Of course, eventually, the grass started growing through the bottom of the plastic liner. In the end, it was like swimming on a grass flat somewhere in Sarasota Bay. All it needed was some salt and a few pinfish and the occasional grunt, maybe a snook or two, and a small tarpon to keep things interesting. I might even have broken out my fly rod and jumped the tarpon every once in a while. I have no idea what a wild trip on acid is like, but if it was anything like my life had been for the past several weeks, someone, please stop the planet. I want to get off. My life was turning into a bad Salvador Dali painting; then again, it could have been a great Salvador Dali painting.

I didn't know what they meant at the time, but my new friends Ricky and Dunning Harvey kept referring to our house as an old conch house, whatever that was, but at least it was on the water. It was on the Grand Canal, which ran in and out of all the various neighborhoods, including the Siesta Key Market area. We lived on the corner of Avenida De Mayo, where it T-boned Avenida Del Norte. The house faced the water and had a small wooden dock that had seen better days, but a dock is a dock, regardless of how rundown it may be. Ralph was always the curious one, and Brandon was always the bitchy one even though I loved him like a brother. Ron, the quiet one, and I spent some time walking around the neighborhood with Ralph and Brandon checking out the local color to get a feel of the place.

The neighborhood, in some ways, reminded me of some of the quirky neighborhoods in Key West and especially the ones on Stock Island. It was kind of comforting, in a strange sort of way. Then again, it could have been nothing more than wishful thinking. It's amazing what you can convince yourself of sometimes. Deep in my heart, I knew it was nothing like Key

West, but maybe more like Haight-Ashbury in the sixties. There is always hope for those of us who never let go of the past.

The only thing missing were the boat people, although a few of the driveways sported flats boats. Aluminum canoes, sometimes stacked three high, sat on worn-out wooden sawhorses under some the carports. Dozens of wet life jackets were hanging on homemade clotheslines, drying in the wind; and what seemed like hundreds of wooden paddles were stacked in the corners.

Ralph and I took a deep breath and just smiled at each other, which is always a good sign. Ralph kept teasing me—he thought I should put a few pictures together and a short bio, then put one in every mailbox, at least the ones that had flats boats in their driveways. From what I could see, it looked like a hippie commune left over from the sixties. Long-haired hippies, surfboards and wet suits, and kids were everywhere. And it seemed like everyone had lots of cats and dogs. For some reason, I felt at home.

At some point, it seems like you should get down on your hands and knees and thank somebody or at least something. It could have been much worse. Every time we passed a house with a for rent or for sale sign in the front yard, Ralph copied down the phone number. I knew it would never happen because he had a thriving guide business in Fort Lauderdale, although I think Ralphs's wife, Linda, would have loved Siesta Key.

Linda was a child of the sixties who wanted nothing to do with the seventies. Linda, bless her soul, still made homemade candles, and she was always giving me some of her homemade soaps. It didn't matter what time it was, day or night; Linda always had plenty of sun tea and cookies. And no, I never asked her what was in the cookies. She always gave you a choice, hot or cold, with or without fresh herbs and lemon. I didn't know whether Brandon would like Sarasota. I think it would have all depended on the nightlife; Brandon always had his priorities in order.

As soon as we unpacked the two pickups, Ralph and the boys said their good-byes and headed back to Fort Lauderdale, but I knew they would never make it back that night. Ralph would work his way back as slowly as possible. I knew Ralph well enough to know that he would fish his way home, and by the time he made it home, he would know the area as well as anyone who lived there. It was in his DNA.

My most immediate problem was where to put all my fishing gear, much less my surfboards. By the time I stuffed everything into my small bedroom, there wasn't much room to sleep in, let alone have a dresser. Eventually, I built a wooden rack on the back side of the house to stack my surfboards. It was far from perfect, but for the moment it would have to do. I was terrified that someone might pilfer my surfboards. I still had the remainder of my boards stashed in Brandon's garage, in case I wanted to run away from home—and that was always a possibility.

Christmas break was almost over. I only had a few days left to explore the surrounding neighborhoods and experience some of the local fishing. On the upside, we only lived several blocks from the beach. All of the roads in the neighborhood led to Beach Road, which ran parallel to Siesta Key Beach. When we first moved to Siesta Key, the island had only a handful of older condos and only one on the beach side.

Monday finally arrived, and I had to enroll in the local middle school. Brookside Middle School was small compared to the old Fort Lauderdale High School. It was an easy process. In fact, I had to start the same day I enrolled. My first class was English, and honestly, the first question I asked the kid sitting next to me was how easy was it to skip school. I think he replied, "Why do you want to skip school?"

I took a deep breath and settled in for a long day. On the way home, I had to take the school bus. Seriously, it was the first time I had ever ridden a school bus. Over the years I had taken the public bus, I had hitchhiked, I had walked, and if nothing else, I just rode my bicycle to school. After that day, I never rode the school bus again, except when I played high school football.

It was a difficult year. Busing was in full swing, and absolutely no one wanted to be bused to another school. There is not enough room in this book to get into the trials and tribulations and the chaos busing caused in the early seventies. I don't think a week went by without riots and fights erupting throughout the school. I was suspended twice and, eventually, expelled for the rest of the school year. A few weeks before school closed for the summer, the principal called my parents and invited me back for the remainder of the year.

Two days later, four or five of us were leaning against the railing outside the principal's office, watching the cheerleaders parade up and down the halls waving pompoms in our faces. Then Ricky pulled out a BIC lighter and lit one of the pompoms on fire. The cheerleader ran down the hall waving the burning pompoms in front of the principal's office. To make a long story short, I was out the door again.

Believe it or not, I passed the ninth grade, and I was headed for Riverview High School. Obviously, the principal recognized my genius and felt I was ready for a higher education—and maybe some intensive discipline.

· *16* ·

The Summer of Discovery

$\mathcal{F}$inally, summer arrived. It had been a rough start to the year so far. But things were about to change. I made friends with several kids in the neighborhood, and a few of them thought they liked to fish until they met me. Up to this point, I had been fishing the canals throughout my neighborhood and had done quite well. Plenty of snook and small tarpon were in the canal across the street from our house. Red fish, spotted sea trout, and ladyfish were everywhere. I fished the beaches for snook in the mornings and early evenings.

It wasn't Anglin's Pier, but I was just getting started, and I hadn't even scratched the surface. The first thing I did was acquire a map of the state of Florida. I folded it in such a way that the only part showing was the west coast. I started highlighting the rivers and passes from the Manatee River in Manatee County to Naples in Collier County in southwest Florida. I was dumbfounded at the number of rivers that flowed to the sea, most via well-known estuaries such as Charlotte Harbor and eventually, into the passes such as Boca Grande.

It was almost intimidating. There was the Manatee River, and the Little Manatee in Manatee County, the Myakka River in Sarasota County, the Peace River and the Caloosahatchee River in Lee County, and dozens of smaller tributaries that flowed into the major estuaries. Of course, most of these rivers were so large they ran through more than one county. Then, the Intracoastal Waterway ran from Tampa Bay and eventually, to the ocean at the south end of Sanibel Island. There were passes such as Longboat Pass in Manatee County; New Pass, Big Pass, and Midnight Pass in Sarasota County; the north and south jetties in Nokomis; Stump Pass in Charlotte County; Little Gasparilla Pass, Boca Grande Pass, Captiva Pass, Redfish Pass, and Blind Pass in Lee County. It seemed endless, and it was essentially all in my backyard. Over the next few years, I fished them all. To make things even better, most of these places were within an hour's drive from my house, some a mere twenty minutes by bicycle.

The number of bridges that cross the Intracoastal Waterway from the Manatee River to the Marco Bridge is astonishing. The bridges that cross the mouth of the passes from the Longboat Pass in Manatee County to the Big San Carlos Pass in Lee County and eventually, the Hickory Pass in Bonita Beach, can be at times some of the most productive bridges in the state of Florida. In fact, the state record snook came from the Big San Carlos Bridge. The bridge tender caught a 44-pound, 3-ounce snook in the draw on a dead tide using a white chicken feather with a white rubber worm as a trailer. Nevertheless, I'm more than sure that that record has been broken several times since then. The two bridges that connected Siesta Key to the mainland in the early seventies, the Siesta Key Bridge on the north end of Siesta Key and the Stickney Point Bridge on the south end, were nothing short of incredible when I arrived. The mouth of Big Pass was a ten-minute walk from my front door.

Big Pass was the largest pass in Sarasota County, and for the most part, it was the major drainage for Sarasota Bay. Access was easy, and the beaches were pristine. Snook were stacked everywhere on the outgoing tide, especially in the late summer and early fall when they were spawning. In May, June, and July, Big Pass was thick with huge tarpon. We could wade the three or four miles of open beach on the south side—bounce plastic bait using popping rods and Ambassadeurs loaded with ten- or twelve-pound test line—and catch sea trout, redfish, and mackerel until our arms cramped. In the right season, and on the right tide, beach fishing was nothing short of cosmic. As fantastic as the fishing could be in the morning, I much preferred to fish for snook at night on the incoming tide.

It was becoming obvious that Sarasota was an undiscovered gem, or at least it was being devoured at a much slower pace than the east coast. For some reason, the massive hordes of refugees from the Northeast and the European tourists preferred the east coast, and the smaller hordes of snowbirds from the Midwest and the Canadians preferred the west coast. How long this would last no one really knew. All I knew is that I wanted to explore it all before it went the way of the dinosaurs. It didn't take a genius to figure this out; even I knew what was headed this way.

Looking back, I could easily have called this the summer of discovery. I think I fished six out of seven days a week, and some weeks I scoured the beaches in the morning and then took a nap, fished the bridges all night, and then hit the beaches again on the way home.

Over the next several years, I would begin to meet some of the most eccentric people you could imagine and some you probably couldn't imagine, or better yet, some you wouldn't want to imagine. Some would fall away for various reasons; others such as Walt Winton, Mark Riehemann, Dick Clevenger, and Ray Moss would last a lifetime. None of them had much in common except maybe me. Unlike Fort Lauderdale, most of my friends were older than I was and set in their ways long before I showed up. It began the first time I fished the Siesta Key Bridge.

Home Is Where the Snook and Tarpon Live

*E*very morning, I would get up early to ride my bike to school so I didn't have to take the bus. Occasionally, my stepfather would give me a ride to school, which usually meant that I either had to take the school bus home or catch a ride with someone who was headed my way. For the most part, I just walked home. It didn't matter how I managed to get there: I had to cross either Siesta Key Bridge or Stickney Point Bridge. I much preferred Siesta Key Bridge on the north end of the island because it was exponentially longer than Stickney Point Bridge. When the sun was high, the water was incredibly clear; you could see the turquoise blue channels that faded to dark navy blues in the deeper channels that crisscrossed the bay in all directions. The white sandy flats that lined the deeper channels glowed in the afternoon sun as if they were fluorescent. The grass flats were smothered in turtle grass. The grass heaved to and fro with the change of the tides, as if they were waving at you when you walked by.

The contrast between the deep blue water in the channels and the brilliant white sandy flats adjacent to the intense greens of the turtle grass seemed surreal. Looking back, it reminded me of the intense breezy colors of a Winslow Homer watercolor, especially the one he painted when he visited South Florida in the wintertime. I didn't know it at the time, but the grass flats were overflowing with shrimp, pass crabs, and a multitude of baitfish and crustaceans. I found out later that the grass flats of Sarasota Bay were once full of clams, queen conchs, stone crabs, and various other spiny epicurean delights. It was unbelievable; Sarasota Bay, at which I was looking, was what remained of a massive dredging project for a man-made island named Bird Key.

The developers, for the most part, built a massive seawall the size of a large island, then they dredged Sarasota Bay for years to obtain the fill. In the process they destroyed the majority of the grass flats and oyster bars in Sarasota Bay, and what grass was left was silted in by all the loose sand. The new man-made island eventually would provide multimillion-dollar homes for the rich and famous.

Later that year, over breakfast, Dick Clevenger would tell me unbelievable stories about the enormous schools of redfish and sea trout that once called Sarasota Bay home. At some point, you would think people would scream out in disgust. Even at a young age, deep in my gut, I knew that would never happen. The combination of corrupt politicians, unsavory attorneys, and greedy developers always seem to win. In every sense of the word, it was disgusting. Why did we let it happen? I can only assume that no one really cared, or if they did care, they were powerless to stop the carnage. Have we really lost the ability to love and respect nature, or at least feel a little empathy for the life of the many splendid creatures that call the oceans home? Obviously, we have, or things like this could never have happened.

I put the Coleman lantern in the cooler and then put the cooler in the basket on the front of my bicycle. I put the five-gallon bucket with the cast net on my handlebars, my rods and dip net in the two baskets on the back. It was six-thirty, maybe seven o'clock in the evening. Several hours of daylight remained.

Thank God a bicycle path kept me off the road. Still, people kept slowing down and staring at me as if I were Don Quixote tilting at windmills. It was slow going at first until the bike sort of reached a point of symmetry and balanced itself out. Traveling north, the first bridge I came to was what people kept calling Humpback Bridge—though I doubt the little bridge had an official name. It had to be one of the shortest bridges on the planet. Literally, only one or two people could fish the bridge at any given time. Parking was scarce. In fact, "no parking" signs were everywhere. The key to Humpback Bridge was that it had an exceptionally bright street lamp on the south side that kept the water lit and provided a great shadow line for snook to lie behind and wait for a fat unsuspecting shrimp to float by.

Once you have a consistent light source, night after night, the bait starts to show up, and when you have bait, the snook and tarpon begin to appear. It's not rocket science. On the north side of the canal, the water dumped directly into Big Pass and eventually ran to the ocean. The bridge was so close to the pass that if you dropped an empty milk jug in the water on an outgoing tide, you could pick it up on the beach side a few minutes later.

Come to find out Siesta Key alone had six, maybe seven, of these small bridges, and they all held snook at the right tide. The right tide was the key, though it seemed like no two bridges shared the same formula. It took years and lots of patience to figure out what the right tide was. Even more confusing, the right tide kept changing, depending on the season. In fact, so many of these small bridges were scattered throughout Sarasota and Venice, you could have made a living just fishing them. Over the years, I think Dick Clevenger and I tried to fish them all at different times and tides throughout the year, all with varying degrees of success. It became as much a game as anything else. I must admit, bridges were so numerous that we started keeping notes; I still have most of them. But the Humpback would have to wait for another day.

One Friday night, I wanted to get to Siesta Key Bridge early in case it was crowded. I had no idea what to expect, what I would do, or where I would fish, or for that matter, what I would fish for. For all practical purposes, I was flying by the seat of my pants. It felt sublime. I always hated schedules and even worse, expectations. I have always found that expectations never bring anything but disappointment. All I really wanted to do that first night was show up, look around, and go with the flow.

That being said, I was never a patient person. When I finally made it to Siesta Key Bridge, cars and trucks were parked everywhere on both sides. I arrived several months before the county planned to start work on the new bridge. Several barges were tied up to the seawall, with two large cranes ready to go to work at the drop of a hat. People along the seawall parked their cars and trucks side by side but several feet from the seawall, as if something were preventing them from pulling up to the edge. They were unfolding plastic chairs and recliners as if they were going to watch a football game. Then it dawned on me: it was an outgoing tide, and they were shrimping.

It was beginning to get dark. Coleman lanterns began to come out, and then they started putting together long three-piece dip nets. In some ways, it was kind of comical to watch; not everyone had the timing and coordination to assemble one. From what I could tell, more than one shrimper that night was thumped upside the head by a clumsy neighbor. It reminded me of the shrimp runs at Anglin's Pier when the shrimp would blow out of Biscayne Bay by the thousands. The shrimpers would stand shoulder to shoulder and fight over a big shrimp floating through the lights. People started calling out "my shrimp, my shrimp," as if they were calling fly balls at a baseball game or trying to hail a cab at Fifth and Pine. It was vicious at times. It's difficult to understand how one lonely shrimp could bring out the worst in humanity.

Still laughing, I chained my bicycle to the guardrail located at the beginning of the bridge. I grabbed the five-gallon bucket with the cast net and my rods and dip net. My hands were full; I could only carry so much fishing gear at one time. Even though I didn't want to, I had to leave the cooler for the next trip. Maybe sixty or seventy people were shrimping. But there couldn't have been more than ten people on the bridge, and they weren't fishing; they were standing around shooting the bull. In some ways, it brought back fond memories of Anglin's Pier.

Because it was summer and school was out, I thought the bridge would be overrun with young kids and a few teenagers who thought they might have been the reincarnation of Joe Brooks. But of course, that was assuming that they even knew who Joe Brooks was. I was so wrong. I didn't see anyone under thirty that night. I went back to my bicycle and dragged my cooler back to the bridge. I had stashed the remainder of my gear about a hundred feet from the draw. When I was walking back up the bridge, I saw three guys admiring my tackle. When I finally reached my rods, one of the three, a rather large person asked me, "What the hell are you supposed to be: a half-assed astronaut or something?"

I had no idea how to answer that question, or if I should say anything. He was huge. One of the other guys, a bald-headed guy with a beer belly, told him to leave me alone. A third guy standing there was just watching. I didn't know what to think; he was of medium build and about my height, slightly overweight. That night he was sporting a worn-out set of work clothes held up by a pair of red suspenders, cowboy boots that had seen better days, a cowboy hat pulled down over his eyes, and a sinister look on his face. Beneath the cowboy hat he had a scrubby mustache with a long, untidy beard. What caught my immediate attention was a giant Bowie knife on his old work belt. He lit a cigarette, smiled, and eventually walked away without saying a word.

As they walked away, I didn't know exactly what had just happened. Either I had just experienced a close encounter with the third kind or the devil's rejects. It was either a science fiction movie gone terribly wrong or a horror movie that would haunt me for the rest of my life. I almost packed up and went back to Humpback Bridge. I remember thinking to myself, *And I thought Fort Lauderdale was weird.*

· 18 ·

Dick Clevenger and the Boys in the Band

$\mathcal{T}$he tide finally started to swing, and at least on the surface, everyone seemed more interested in the fishing than in me. At that time, I was more interested in walking around the bridge and meeting everyone, getting the lay of the land. The tide changed, and the shrimpers started to disperse in all directions, unfortunately at the same time. It looked like the parking lot at the Orange Bowl after a Miami Dolphins football game. I took my lantern and dip net along with a five-gallon bucket with a new aerator down to the sea wall. I started pumping up the lantern until the pressure was so high, I couldn't push in the plunger anymore.

I turned the valve on high and lit the match, then gingerly, and I mean gingerly, put the match in the hole under the glass. When the mantles finally started to burn, it almost exploded. I knew it would. It always scared me; if it didn't, I would have thought something was wrong. An old military lantern that was used in Vietnam and in the Korean War, it was so bright that it was almost obnoxious.

The common name for the fuel was unleaded kerosene, but it was akin to nitromethane, the same fuel used in high-performance dragsters and funny cars. The downside to unleaded kerosene was that it would burn through new mantles like they were paper. The Coleman mantles lasted one, maybe two nights at best. I still have one of the old lanterns hanging up in my den, but I don't think I would ever try to light it again. I would like to keep my hair, at least what hair I still have left.

I held the lantern as close as I could to the edge of the seawall to see what I could see. I hoped I would find a few leftover shrimp. Traditionally, shrimp only run on an outgoing tide and only if the water temperature is warm enough. A full moon is always better because of the stronger tides.

Shrimp tend to gather at the mouths of passes and lay their eggs. Somewhere in the process, the eggs are fertilized and hatched, and the juvenile shrimp eventually find their way back on an incoming tide to the same grass flats where they started. On a slack tide, they drop back and settle in the grass and wait out the incoming tide until another outgoing tide is strong enough to carry them to sea. Depending on the water temperature and the weather conditions, you could find shrimp throughout the summer almost anywhere in the subtropics, especially in South Florida.

A great way to dip shrimp is to jump off the seawall and wade the grass flats with a miner's light on your head. Every time you see two orange eyes, slip the net under them and move on to the next pair. Sometimes it's much easier than sitting on the seawall and waiting for them to float by. It's also an excellent way to pick up a few flounder. Looking back, I seem to have spent an enormous part of my life on a grass flat somewhere, chasing everything from shrimp to permit. Fishing the flats at night, especially by yourself, can be a spiritual awakening. If you're wading the right flat at the right tide, during a full moon, the fishing can be cosmic. At times, the solitude can be deafening, but you will never experience a more intimate relationship with nature—especially if you are wading barefooted. You never know what might go bump in the dark.

As soon as I started combing the seawall, I started seeing shrimp everywhere. Until the tide changed, the shrimp were floating throughout the water column using the current like a conveyer belt. Now, they were desperately clinging to the barnacles and small oysters that had cemented themselves to the seawalls. At this point, the last thing the shrimp needed to do was lose ground to the incoming tide. All I had to do was scoop them up with my dip net. When I had a dozen or so in the net, I emptied the net into the bucket. I eventually made my way around the corner and found myself under the bridge. A shallow sandbar snaked its way between the pilings and the seawall. It seemed at the time a great place to explore. I jumped off the seawall and waded in up to my knees with the lantern. When I finally made it to where the grass started, shrimp were everywhere.

I must have netted three or four dozen in the next half hour, too many to keep alive in the same five-gallon bucket. My aerator just wasn't strong enough. I set the lantern on the seawall, put more water in the bucket, lifted it up, and set it beside the lantern. Then I tried to jump back up on the seawall. It wasn't much fun, but I finally made it. My knees were bleeding, my elbows were scratched, and my lower lip was bloody, but it seemed like a small price to pay for all the shrimp. In the end, it was a toss-up. If I had known how hard it would be getting back up on the seawall, I am not sure I would have jumped down in the first place. But then again, one does need bait.

I dragged myself up on the bridge and started cleaning my knees when the cowboy walked up and asked what I had. At that point, I told him the whole story and showed him all the shrimp. Then he asked if I needed another bucket and aerator. I thought that was a nice gesture, but I also thought I had just given this goofy-looking cowboy half my shrimp. He finally introduced himself: Dick Clevenger. Little did I know that over the next thirty-five years or so, we would be as close as any father and son on this planet could be, maybe even closer.

He finally introduced me to Wally and Lew. Wally was the giant, and Lew was the bald-headed man with the beer belly. It reminded me of the Magnificent Seven, except there were only four guns for hire instead of seven. Of course, I imagined myself as Yul Brynner for no other reason than he didn't get shot.

After a few minutes, I moved my fishing gear next to theirs. From that point on, we were almost inseparable. The next morning, we packed up all our gear and went our separate ways. This went on for the next several weeks, and eventually, Dick asked where I lived, so I gave him my address—why, I have no idea. I still wasn't sure that Dick wasn't the reincarnation of Charlie Manson or some other unsavory character you see on the evening news.

Several days later, out of the blue, Dick pulled up in front of our house, driving an old, beat-up, rusty Ford Maverick. It was burning oil, probably at the same rate it was guzzling gas. Until that day, I didn't think a four-cylinder engine could guzzle gas. Then again, what did I know; I was still riding a bicycle. I had to hand it to Dick: he cleaned up before he came over, or let's just say Dick cleaned up as much as he wanted to clean up.

For some reason, Dick left his cowboy hat at home and ditched the Bowie knife. I didn't think about it at the time, but he probably stashed the knife under the front seat. We were on the front porch talking about the canal across the street. I was starting to tell him about the snook and small tarpon in the canal when my mom opened the screen door and introduced herself. Eventually, my stepfather came out and joined the conversation.

I don't remember much about the conversation, but my parents invited him in for dinner. Somewhere between the fried chicken and the mashed potatoes, he explained to my parents that it didn't make much sense for me to keep riding my bicycle back and forth to the bridge every weekend. He would be happy to pick me up and bring me home. It never dawned on me that I would have to ride in that piece of junk in the front yard. I could only hope that Wally or Lew had a car or a truck of their own. My parents seemed to think this was a great idea. I could only assume that I was on my own the other five days. Dick and my parents became close friends, and over the years, he took care of our house and yard. Years later, he built a beautiful pool cage for my parents' new home. Anything that needed fixing—Dick could fix it.

Friday finally arrived, and Dick showed up at six-thirty that night. I had my gear stacked up against the garage door. Dick climbed out of his car and walked up to the porch. He just stood there for a moment, staring at all my tackle. Then he looked back at his car, then my tackle. The first question out of his mouth was, "Why do you need so much tackle?"

I knew this was a debate I wouldn't win. My question was, how much can I take? He just shrugged his shoulders and started loading my gear. In the end, I had to leave a few rods and a cooler at the house, but I did manage to stuff quite a bit of fishing gear in what little room Dick had left for me. Getting in and out of the car was an adventure, a problem with which I was well acquainted. I had been down this road many times before.

Finally, we were on the road; of course, the Siesta Key Bridge was only a few minutes away. When we reached the bridge, I expected Dick to stop and pull in the parking lot. Instead, he kept going, where, I had no idea. All I knew is that we were heading north on US 41. At this point, I will spare you all the rights and lefts, ups and downs it takes to get to Hart's Landing from Siesta Key. It wouldn't make much sense anyway because everything's changed. When we finally pulled in, we noticed Wally and Lew sitting at one of the washed-out picnic tables having a few beers. I remember a big plywood sign above the bait house in big red letters that read "Hart's Landing."

Dick and I climbed out of the Maverick, waved at Wally and Lew, and then headed up to the bait house. Actually, I think I waved at Wally and Lew. I think Dick gave them the middle finger.

Instead of ordering bait through the front window like most honest people, Dick just opened the side door, walked in, and grabbed a couple of beers from the fridge, as if he owned the place. He then introduced me to Dennis, the real owner. Dennis smiled, shook my hand, and offered a beer. I said, "Sure." Dick chimed in, "He is only fourteen—give the kid a Pepsi."

Later, I learned that Dick's father and Deamus Hart, aka Old Man Hart, had grown up together in Sarasota. They were both commercial fishermen. Dick was never too keen on first names. In fact, he was married twice, and both his wives had the same name: Mother.

· *19* ·

The Patron Saint of Hart's Landing

*O*ld Man Hart started his rather meager bait business in 1934 on a sandy spit on Golden Gate Point long before the John Ringling Causeway was built. According to legend, he owned several hundred feet of seine nets and a bottle of Jack Daniels. He would start a fire on the beach to attract the shrimp, then use the seine net to catch the shrimp and the bottle of Jack to console himself. Fishermen would pull up to buy shrimp, and Old Man Hart would have to wade out and dip about three dozen shrimp at a time, give or take a few, from the collapsed seine net. He put the shrimp in the fishermen's bucket and charged the guys two bits.

In 1964 the Ringling Causeway was finished, and he moved his operation a few feet down the beach to where it sits now. Years later, Dennis, only thirteen years old at the time, started working in the shop with his father. Dick and Dennis grew up together until Dick ran away from home and joined Ringling Bros. and Barnum & Bailey Circus at fourteen. For some reason, that didn't surprise me much.

Over the years, I heard this story hundreds of times, and it seemed to change every time Dick reminisced about the days of his youth, changing just enough to make you think it was a new story. All I know for sure was that Dick and Dennis grew up together, Dick's father and Old Man Hart knew each other, and Old Man Hart started his small bait business in 1934 on Golden Gate Point. From that point on the story evolved over the next thirty years. But, of course, in the long run, it didn't matter. But, if you knew Dick Clevenger well enough, you knew he was full of great stories, and most of them probably were true.

On the other hand, you didn't want to get Dick started on anything pertaining to Bigfoot or the Lost City of Atlantis. If by chance he started talking about UFOs and pyramids, you might as well call it a night. Dick loved the pseudo-sciences. He wasn't exactly a tale spinner because, in some ways, I think he believed his own stories. If nothing else, that should let him off the hook. Dick was always entertaining, sometimes to a fault, and if you happened to be bored, all you had to do was wind him up like a toy soldier and stand back.

Dick finally went back to his car and grabbed a couple of five-gallon buckets he had pilfered from Mister Donut. He started filling the buckets with water, then sifted his way through the treasure trove of shrimp in the bait tank. He was only interested in handpicks, especially the ones that were faster than he was. Dick didn't have to pay for bait; I found out later that he had been catching and supplying bait for Hart's Landing for the past fifteen years, so he had free rein there any time, day or night.

Every once in a while, Dick would take out Dennis's small boat to dredge the grass flats for shrimp, even though Dick hated doing it because he always ended up with more slimy catfish than shrimp. Then it would take him hours to clean the catfish out of the nets. Even worse, Dick got seasick in the bathtub.

It was starting to get dark, and I wondered when we might get to fish. Little did I know at the time, but they hadn't even talked about where we were going to fish. A kind of tribal ritual, it went the same way every Friday and Saturday night.

· 20 ·

Patience Is a Virtue, My Young Padawan

*P*atience is an art form—an acquired taste. It's a taste few teenagers have, much less practice. I could only be patient for so long. It was almost nine o'clock, the sun was about to go down, and we were still sitting around the picnic table trying to decide where to fish that night.

From their cryptic conversation, it looked like we would leave Hart's, have dinner at a place called the Clock Restaurant in Venice, then fish our way back to Sarasota. Believe me when I tell you that I am not opposed to a good meal in the middle of the night, but how much time does it take to put together a plan? The more I tried to motivate these three, the more it looked like we might be sitting at the same picnic table when the sun peeked over the horizon. I was about to take a bait bucket, a few shrimp, and my spinning rod to fish the causeway while they decided what they wanted to do.

When Dick finally asked me if I was ready to leave, I said I wasn't in any hurry. But, of course, he knew I was being a smart ass. Finally, we were headed in the right direction, wherever that might be, but at least we were moving. I hopped in Dick's old Maverick, and Wally jumped in Lew's new Ford pickup. Dick had a hard time keeping up with Lew, but he didn't seem to mind. Dick approached life at his own pace. And if you didn't like it, you could always walk.

Nothing about Mr. Clevenger was ordinary—he lived in his own quirky world, and he rarely invited anybody else in. The upside is that after meeting Dick, not too many people wanted to visit that world. The Maverick's small four-cylinder was making so much noise you couldn't hear the AM radio, much less converse. We were heading south on US 41, and according to the map on my bedroom wall, Venice was only twelve or thirteen miles south of Sarasota. I was worried that I wouldn't have enough money for breakfast, much less enough left to chip in for gas.

What makes a grown man wear a cowboy hat and keep a Bowie knife strapped to his leg? On the surface, Dick was one of the nicest people I have ever met. I couldn't imagine him using the Bowie knife on anyone or anything. Maybe it was part of his self-image. I mean, why did kids dye their hair green and purple? Why did teenagers show up at school strutting a new Mohawk? I had no idea. Maybe it was just a phase, but I doubted it. I think deep down, that's how Dick pictured himself. Then again, just because he was a nice guy on the surface didn't mean he wasn't a homicidal maniac underneath.

Years later, I found out that his first wife had died of prolonged cancer and had spent the last several months of her life in the hospital. It broke his heart. In the end, his insurance company only covered a tiny portion of the bills, and Dick had to declare bankruptcy. I don't think he ever recovered emotionally or financially. At fourteen, you don't have much insight into adults and how difficult life can be. It wasn't hard to see that Dick had lived a rough life, and I didn't see it getting much better any time soon. Life will never be right for some people.

I might have been making too big a deal about all of this. In reality, Dick and the boys had their act together. They had been playing this game for a long time, and they probably knew the ins and outs of every bridge from Tampa Bay to Boca Grande and every dock light in between. It wasn't a challenging game to play in the early seventies. I can only imagine what it must have been like in the fifties and sixties—or better yet, at the turn of the century. The early 1900s had to be cosmic, that is, until you realize they didn't have mosquito repellent, much less air conditioning. I have always been amazed that any of Florida's early settlers managed to survive the harsh Florida landscape, much less flourish.

It didn't matter which bridge you planned to fish; snook literally were stacked like cordwood from end to end. You could stand on almost any bridge and see hundreds, if not thousands of snook most of the time. If the fender had a decent light on the end, you could spot fish in the twenty- to thirty-pound range sitting there with their noses pointed into the current. Then again, if you were lucky, sometimes you could bribe the bridge tender to turn on the lights under the bridge. Then things got insane. The snook would start to stack up in the draw; at some point, the bait would start to ball up, and then the massacre would begin. It was almost too easy.

Of course, the larger fish were the most challenging to catch. If you were using live shrimp for bait, it was difficult to keep the smaller fish away. I have no idea why, but for some inexplicable reason, some bridges were stacked with smaller snook, whereas others were well known for leviathans. Over the next several years, I found that the bridges that straddled the passes always held huge snook. I think it was because there was so much more bait, and the bait always seemed larger. The passes invariably were full of silver mullet and tons of big threadfins and various other types of pilchards and ladyfish. The last thing I had to worry about that night was catching a few snook.

You have to remember that most of the fish we fished for were migratory species, especially the gamefish. For the most part, snook migrated east and west, not north and south, at least not for any considerable distance. Most of the snook we would be fishing for that night had spent the winter months far up in the rivers away from the cold fronts that came blasting down the west coast during December and January. They had spent the past winter deep in the freshwater rivers south of Tampa Bay. Once the temperature dropped below seventy degrees, the snook started to fall back in increments of a few degrees at a time. Of course, I can give you dozens of situations where you can still catch big snook in brackish water during the summer months, especially in the rainy season. And if you happen to live near a spillway, anything is possible.

Snook fishing became predictable once you learned the ins and outs. Then you just had to understand the relationship between a snook and the tides, and why one bridge fishes better on an incoming tide and another on an outgoing tide. Unless you have all the time in the world, it's best to fish with someone who's been chasing snook for a long time, especially big snook. That's where I found myself that night. I was in the hands of three guys who might not have been much to look at, but together they represented sixty, maybe seventy years of snook fishing in a reasonably small undeveloped region of Florida. At least that's what they kept telling me.

At this point, all I knew for sure was that they were exceptionally good at wolfing down pancakes and bacon and drinking endless cups of coffee. We were getting ready to pay the bill when Lew picked up the check and paid the tab. That worked out well. If Dick stopped for gas, I could chip in a few bucks.

Before we started our slow, agonizing retreat north, Dick wanted to check out two bridges in Venice: the Circus Bridge and the Venice Avenue Bridge. If we had time, we might run over to the Venice Pier. I kept thinking about Napoleon's long, miserable retreat west through the snow and ice from Moscow. It didn't work out so well for Napoleon. By this time, I had given up hope of fishing that night. Later, Lew told me to have patience: they wanted to fish the old Englewood Bridge on the tide change, then follow the tide changes north and fish Stickney Point and Siesta Key Bridge. I had to think long and hard about that. I wasn't sure the tides worked that way. There wasn't that much difference between the time the tide changed in Venice and Sarasota Bay.

That night I found out that if we pulled up to a bridge and left the fishing gear in the car, we probably wouldn't fish. It was nothing more than an excuse for low-level reconnaissance.

Two Spiral Galaxies and One Black Hole

Lew was an odd sort of guy but in a good way. If I had to choose between Dick, Wally, and Lew, I would have to say Lew was probably the most normal of the three, if you consider someone who makes false teeth for a living normal. Lew was married, though I don't remember meeting his wife. I waved at her a few times from the car, but I don't remember Lew introducing us. Lew always lived on the fringe of the group. He would show up now and then, or whenever his wife gave him permission.

On the way to the Circus Bridge, I asked Dick how many nights a week he managed to fish. For some reason, Dick only fished on the weekends. He would get off work around four o'clock on Friday afternoon, deposit his paycheck, and then pick up "Mother" to take her grocery shopping and then to dinner. After dinner, Dick would drop Mother off at the house, head down to Hart's Landing, and have a few beers. Then he would fish all night and end up at Hart's on Saturday morning for coffee and doughnuts.

Mr. Clevenger was a man set in his ways. It didn't matter if it was raining, it didn't matter if it was freezing, or in the middle of a hurricane—his routine never varied. He had an agreement with Mother, and he was terrified that if he changed his routine, even once, she might find a crack in his airtight contract. The last thing Dick wanted to do was set such a precedent. Years later, a friend of mine, Walt Winton, stopped by the Venice Pier on a stormy night and saw Dick's van in the parking lot. It was the only vehicle in the lot, so he decided to see what Dick was up to. As he walked under the sheltered area of the pier, he saw Dick wrapped up in his sleeping bag, sound asleep on a concrete bench. I have no idea what it would take to make Dick go home on a Friday or Saturday night. I often found him in his van sound asleep at Hart's Landing.

Wally, on the other hand, was an oxymoron waiting to happen. Wally was huge by anyone's standard, but he didn't seem to eat much. He rarely worked because he didn't have to. His father had set up a trust fund that would provide for Wally and his mother for the rest of their lives. At one time or another, his father had owned a tremendous amount of land in upstate New York and eventually sold some or most of it to the Boy Scouts of America.

Wally always seemed to have two or three boats at one time. He loved to fish, but he also loved to stand around on the bridges and shoot the bull. Compared to Dick and Lew, he was an exceptional fisherman, but he never fished that much; and if he did fish, he never did it in a hurry. Wally was one of the few people I knew who had as much fishing tackle or more than I did. Fishing was a social event for Wally, and this night was no different. We walked out of the Clock Restaurant and stood in the parking lot for another half hour, rehashing everything we had decided to do. At some point, I thought we might go back into the restaurant for dessert and another cup of coffee. I have to admit, it wouldn't have taken much coaxing. According to Dick, the Clock was well known for its peach cobbler and ice cream.

We changed the batteries in the aerators so that the shrimp wouldn't die and eventually made our way to the pier. It wasn't like any pier I had ever seen: it was in the middle of nowhere. The deck was built low to the water, the railings seemed to be at the right height, and it had ample lighting everywhere. We walked out on the pier, and of course, the boys knew everyone. Dick introduced me to everyone he knew. I don't want to make too big a deal about this, but some odd people were on the pier that night.

Once we made it to the tee, it was tough to walk around without tripping over all the shark rods, dozens of coolers, rolled-up sleeping bags, and dead bait lying on the deck. Dick introduced me to a squirrelly sort of guy named Spiderman—no, I didn't think that was his real name. An even stranger gentleman was Harry, who introduced me to his wife, Mary, and that's all I will say about Mary. Some things are better left to the imagination.

Over the years, Harry and I became close friends. What I remember most about Harry was that he was always dependable. You could call him day or night, and Harry would show up. He was generous to a fault. I can't say that about many people. Mary went home, and Harry went to the old Englewood Bridge with us. Harry laid carpet by trade. He had a full-size Ford van, which more often than not, was broken down somewhere on US 41 between Fort Myers and Sarasota. When we finally left the pier, we looked like a half-assed convoy: a Ford pickup loaded with fishing gear, a Ford van carrying twenty rolls of carpet, and one ratty old Ford Maverick burning oil. It almost sounded like a bad country and western song.

The area had very little development at that time, and it was completely dark when we arrived. The old Englewood Bridge was an incredible piece of history: when the city or county decided to build the new bridge, they cut the draw out of the old one and turned what was left into two fishing piers. The new bridge was about fifty yards to the north. At the time, it didn't have any lights on it either. Usually, that was the opposite of what you were looking for if you expected to catch a few snook. It's not someplace I would have stopped to fish if I had been by myself.

Finally, I understood why Dick carried a giant Bowie knife. He told me the old Englewood Bridge was legendary for monster snook. The trick was a great lantern and a strong outgoing tide. The parking lot was more like a grass field loaded with potholes and broken pieces of the original draw and rusted cable. Two old pickups were already parked in the grass, and when Dick saw them, he just started cussing in all directions. Safe to say, the boys knew who these guys were, and they didn't seem to like them very much. One pickup had the skull of a thirty-pound snook mounted on the hood as an ornament. Both vehicles had old beat-up camper shells and homemade canoe racks to which were lashed several long bamboo poles. Later, Harry told me the bamboo poles were used for something called stirring. Old-timers loved to lie on their bellies on a bridge or a pier with long Calcutta poles, a short piece of heavy line, and a homemade plug made of balsa wood, then turn figure eights on the surface of the water. The snook could take the teasing for just so long. Eventually, they crashed the wooden plug and tried to rip it to shreds.

The boys didn't seem very excited anymore. We walked out on the bridge, and sure enough, the two idiots Dick kept telling me about were walking two propane lanterns slowly toward each other. Wally kept telling me, "You have to see this—you're never going to believe it."

They were walking so slowly that I didn't think they would ever meet in the middle. It's nothing more than simple math—there is absolutely no positive number you can't divide by two, and if you keep dividing by two, the increments get smaller and smaller, but the two objects will never touch. Of course, I think I was the only one on the bridge who might have understood simple math. When I finally got to look over the railing, it was impressive. I wouldn't say I was shocked, but I saw something I had never seen or even heard of before.

A giant ball of bait and dozens of snook were under each lantern. The two propane lanterns were on a collision course. It reminded me of two spiral galaxies, the Milky Way and Andromeda, each with a massive black hole at its center, spiraling out of control. They were heading toward each other at unbelievable speeds, with the inevitable bound to happen: mutual mass destruction of both galaxies. In the end, they would form one giant galaxy, and the same sort of collision was coming to the two balls of bait. The difference was that once the two balls collided, one of the scumbags (at least that's what Dick liked to call them) was about to extinguish the sun. When the sun went out, the bait exploded in all directions, the snook went ballistic, and both scumbags hooked up simultaneously.

At the time, I didn't know what to think. On the one hand, it was the coolest thing I had ever seen; on the other hand, it seemed to be one step short of chumming. I didn't know whether I felt this way because the boys couldn't stand the two scumbags, or they were fuming mad at the two guys because they hadn't gotten there first.

Later, I found out the two didn't live on the coast but inland sixty or seventy miles in Arcadia, an old cracker town. I couldn't remember where I had heard that name before. Then it dawned on me: Arcadia was a cow town that barely had a population large enough to count, but on the other hand, the state's largest rodeo was held there every year. If I remember right, Arcadia had been the capital of Florida at one time. Today, Tallahassee is Florida's capital, and Arcadia is nothing more than a rundown cow town.

Dick told me his two buddies on the bridge would catch their limit on the early tide, then take the fish back to Arcadia. Later they would drive back to catch the late tide. Even today, I can't figure out why two derelict old fishermen trying to put food on the table bothered me so much. Maybe at some level, it never bothered me. In theory, they weren't doing anything wrong except keeping too many snook, but then again, not all that long ago people just left snook on the bridge to die. At that time, snook were known as soap fish because they tasted like laundry soap. They tasted that way because people didn't fillet the fish in those days. They just scaled them; if you left the skin on a snook, it tasted very much like soap.

Considering how poor some of these fishermen were, it spoke volumes about the taste. Snook had to taste really bad for these guys to leave that many fish to die. Fast-forward a few years, and people started filleting fish. In the process, someone decided to fillet a snook one night, and the rest is history. Today, the snook is one of the most prized table fish in South Florida. But, of course, in the end, it didn't matter. Overdevelopment, overpopulation, and pollution would eventually wipe out most of the snook and eradicate the environment in which they once flourished.

We slowly strolled back to the parking lot as if we were kicking a can down the road. Finally, we jumped in the vehicles and headed north, everybody but Harry. He wasn't sure his van would make it to Sarasota and back to Venice. He said his good-byes and headed south, back to Mary.

It was a little after one in the morning, and I hadn't even picked up a rod yet. So, we decided to skip Stickney Point Bridge and head back to Siesta Key

Bridge. By the time we got there, the tide should be ripping. Hopefully, the bridge would be empty, and we wouldn't have to deal with anything except the late-night bar traffic. The coffee and doughnuts at Hart's were starting to sound good. When we finally pulled into the parking lot at Siesta Key Bridge, we only saw one or two cars in the parking lot. And yes, Dick knew both of them. It was a long bridge, and we had plenty of room. All you needed to do to find snook was take a quick look over the railing and pick your line. Most of the snook you could see were on the small side. The bigger fish were always in deeper channels closer to the draw.

The silence was almost too much to endure. Every few minutes, a car might come over the bridge and honk its horn as it went by. It was so quiet that I could hear the incoming tide and the occasional ladyfish and sea trout popping shrimp on the surface.

If this had been Fort Lauderdale at one in the morning, the bridge would have been packed. The cars would have been backed up for miles trying to get to the beach, horns honking and half-naked girls screaming, pulling up their tops to show off their breasts even though most still had on their bras. Occasionally, some beautiful girl, or worse—a teenage boy—might moon you; you never knew in Fort Lauderdale. I can't tell you how many times I had empty beer bottles thrown at me. On a good night, if you were lucky, one of the crazy kids in the cars might offer you a beer.

The west coast was not only geographically on the opposite side of the state, but it was an alternate universe, one so different it was almost unrecognizable. I missed Fort Lauderdale, my friends, and Anglin's Pier. I wasn't sure that I could ever forgive my parents for moving.

We fished the Siesta Key Bridge until the tide ran out. We even fished the change for a few minutes, but the morning sun was getting higher, and Dick had to get home. We caught a few nice fish that night, nothing to brag about, but at least Dick had a few fish to take home to Mother, and if we didn't leave now, all the coffee and doughnuts would be gone by the time we made it to Hart's. Regardless of that fact, we passed three different doughnut shops on the way to Hart's, all of which probably had great doughnuts. I had no idea what was so special about the doughnuts at Hart's. Come to find out, Hart's was like the Patio on Saint Armand's Circle. Even people who didn't fish showed up at Hart's on Saturday and Sunday mornings. And yes, the doughnuts tasted great, but the company made them taste even better. I should have understood that intuitively, on so many different levels. During my second cup of coffee, I realized that everything would be fine.

I had found a new home.

• 22 •

Good Karma and Positive Energy

$\mathcal{S}$o it went for the next several months.

Dick would pick me up on Friday and Saturday nights, and the four of us either drifted north or south, depending on the tides and the weather. During the week, I continued to fish the beaches. It seemed like a great time to dig out my fly rod, and for the next several weeks, I started using it almost exclusively on the beaches and in the maze of canals that ran in and out of our neighborhood. I was getting to the point where I enjoyed using a fly rod again.

At some point you have to come to terms with a fly rod, stop worrying about your casting technique, and start fishing. When you finally arrive at that stage, it becomes fun. Hooking and landing a fish becomes second nature. But I have to admit, it's not for everyone. It takes a lot of time, energy, and effort to become a good fly fisherman. It can get expensive, and not everyone has the coordination or the temperament. In the end, it's just another way to catch a fish. It's not good or bad, but it can be a tremendous amount of fun, and isn't that's what fishing is supposed to be about?

Believe it or not, Siesta Key had several surf shops. One was down the street in what the locals called the Village, only a few blocks from my house. The other surf shop was at the other end of the island, a few blocks south of the Stickney Point Bridge. I was amazed when Steve Anderson first told me about them. I had met Steve a few weeks earlier. He was in his front yard, cleaning his boat and washing down his truck, trying desperately to scrub off all the salt. I waved. The next thing I knew, we were firing up the grill. A few minutes later, his wife, Wendy, came out the front door carrying a plate of spareribs. A few seconds behind Wendy, their daughter,

Mary, came walking out toting a cooler full of Heinekens. I chalked it up to good living and karma.

I had no idea how the surf shop could make any money. I crawled out of bed every morning and made my way to the beach. And every morning, the Gulf of Mexico was always flat as a pancake, maybe flatter. At least a pancake has a few bumps and a few bubbles, occasionally nooks and crannies, to capture the melted butter and syrup. One morning I stopped by the surf shop in the Village, a few blocks from Siesta Beach. I can't tell you what I expected when I walked through the door, but I was impressed.

O'Hara's was a well-stocked little operation. By the looks of the small shop, it probably sold more T-shirts and boogie boards than surfboards. I walked in like I was Gerry Lopez. That might have been an insult to the real Gerry Lopez, maybe a little over the top, but I had been surfing since I was eight or nine years old. I jumped my first boogie board when I was five or six. Until that time, I had surfed just about everything Florida had to throw at me, including a few hurricanes. It was simple. If there was a decent break, I was surfing; if not, I was fishing.

The bell on the door was still ringing when I walked in, and the smell just about knocked me off my feet. It was one I had smelled hundreds of times, a combination of reefer, surf wax, and resin. O'Hara's was a respite from the norm, a clan, a tribe of kindred spirits, a place to let your hair down. I was most emphatically a child of two very different worlds. Two guys with long hair walked out of the backroom, obviously in a good mood considering the scents wafting through the shop. They looked like they lived on the beach, and from the looks of their tans and sun-bleached hair, they rarely left it. Assuming these were the two guys Steve had told me about, and that was a very big if, they shaped their boards, and one of them had competed in the now-defunct IPS Challenge (International Professional Surfing League) the previous year and had done quite well.

He didn't place, but it was enough to be invited in the first place. I introduced myself and asked the obvious question, "Where the hell do you surf around here?"

Gavin introduced himself and then just started laughing. He was a big kid, probably still in his late teens. By the size of his shoulders and triceps, Gavin had spent most of his life face down on a board paddling, unlike his sidekick, Peter. When I first met Peter, he looked like one of the up-and-coming hot dogs you see on the circuit these days, small boards, all balls, no brains. I was wrong. Peter was sort of philosophical about surfing. The connection between Peter and the waves and nature seemed to be the driving force behind his surfing, not fame and fortune. Years later, he could have played Bodhi in *Point Break*, as in the Bodhisattva. Out of compassion, an enlightened being forgoes nirvana to save others.

Then Peter asked, "How long have you lived here?"

Like a smart ass, I said, "Long enough to know that there hasn't been a wave over two feet in the last six months."

Then both of them chimed in at the same time, "There's no surf anywhere around here."

"Then why do you have two surf shops on Siesta Key?"

It seemed like a reasonable question at the time.

Sarcastically laughing at me or with me, tough to tell which at the time, Gavin replied, "We spend most of our time surfing up and down the East Coast from Virginia to Sebastian Inlet. When we have the opportunity, we love to surf places along the California coast, places like Mavericks in Northern California. Lately, we have been surfing on some of the beaches on the Osa Peninsula in Costa Rica."

That made a lot of sense. At the time, most of the IPS Challenge was normally held in California or Hawaii.

At that point, all I wanted to do was lower my head, sneak out the back door, and pretend this conservation had never taken place. Instead, I found myself in over my head, and at the same time, I wanted to know when the next bus left for Mavericks, even though it was so far out of my league. For all intents and purposes, I didn't have a gun big enough to surf Mavericks or a wet suit thick enough to survive the freezing water. Most of my surfboards were relatively short, high-performance boards made for speed and maneuverability for the smaller waves on the East Coast, not a sixty-foot monster that comes barreling down out of the North Pacific.

But, for some reason, I liked O'Hara's. It reminded me of some of the local shops on the East Coast. I started hanging around O'Hara's a lot that summer, and during the winter months, I worked part-time now and then when Peter and Gavin took off for the West Coast. When they surfed Sebastian and Cocoa Beach, I usually went with them if I didn't have a football game that night. One does need a fix now and then.

You never know what happens when you take the first step and walk through the front door. Sometimes your life can change in an instant. Best of all, I found a home for my wayward surfboards. Life has always been about good karma, strict adherence to feng shui, and positive energy in your daily life. Maybe that's the surfer coming out in me, or maybe it's just another way of saying I got lucky.

It was time to make hay. In two weeks, I had to start an intensive weight-training program at Riverview High School for six weeks, and then the football practices began—two practices a day for another four weeks before the fall semester started. What a miserable way to spend four long weeks, as if July and August in South Florida weren't bad enough. It was a new team, a new coaching staff, and a new school to make things even worse.

On the upside, I had a birthday coming in a few weeks; I would be fifteen years old. For the first time, I was looking forward to going to school. I had signed up for driver's education, which meant that by the end of the semester, I should have a newly minted restricted license. It would be a busy fall.

• 23 •

A Love Affair with Books

$\mathcal{W}$hen I was growing up, I don't think we had a book in the house, not even a Bible. Except for the few fishing magazines I had lying around, no one in my family read anything except the *Sarasota Herald-Tribune*, our local newspaper. I read the sports section, my stepfather read the comics, and God only knows what my mother read if she read anything. A few weeks later, I was in the Sarasota Public Library with a couple of close friends, and, I ended up with a library card. I was with two cheerleaders I had gone to school with the previous year who were working on a high school project they got conned into that summer, something about an Advanced Placement program. I asked the librarian at the reference desk where I might find the sports section, but what I really wanted was the fishing section. Instead, she politely introduced me to the card catalog.

Wherever I went, she kept staring at me, as if I were going to abscond with the family jewels. But, of course, it might have been the way I was dressed. We had just left the beach a few hours before, and all I had on was an old baseball hat, a baggy T-shirt, a pair of worn-out shorts, and a relatively new pair of flip-flops. OK, maybe I didn't look like your run-of-the-mill scholar, but someday my taxes would be paying her salary.

Twenty or thirty minutes later, I found the fishing section—it was huge. Who knew? That day I checked out four great fishing books, at least what I perceived to be great fishing books, though at the time I didn't have the slightest idea who the authors were. I checked out *Fishing with Ray Bergman* by Ray Bergman, *The Fireside Book of Fishing* by Raymond Camp, *The Joys of Trout* by Arnold Gingrich, and *The Complete Guide to Fishing Across North America* by Joe Brooks. I know it sounds a little over the top, but by the time I had finished reading those four books, they had fundamentally changed my life forever. For the first time, I knew what I wanted to do for the rest of my days. Regardless of what I was doing at the time, I knew it would have to revolve around fishing.

It was also the beginning of a lifetime love affair with books. I became a closet bibliophile. It's not something you usually share with your friends. Over the next several months, I lived at the public library, and when school started that year, I devoured the small school library. I was always on the lookout for books that had something to do with steelhead, Atlantic salmon, bonefish, permit, or tarpon. I would burn through books by A. J. McClane, Joe Brooks, Charlie Waterman, Ted Williams, and Lefty Kreh. Later I discovered Roderick Haig-Brown's *The Seasons of a Fisherman* and John Voelker's *Trout Madness*, incredible books that eventually pushed me off the cliff. I was a hard-core junkie. I was mainlining books, and my drug of choice was travel books that had something to do with fishing. I wanted to fish the world. In a small way, I did; if not in person, in my dreams, and I am still trying.

My birthday came and went without much fanfare. I got a few clothes and some spare cash to throw around. I wanted to start rewrapping some of my snook rods, and I knew Dick loved wrapping rods. Even though it took him three times longer than most people because he didn't have a rod-wrapping table, he wrapped everything by hand. I figured Dick was probably strapped for cash, so I picked up the new guides and thread. When he showed up Friday night, I made sure we went over everything. Then I put the guides and thread into a plastic bag so that Dick wouldn't lose anything. I left the original cork and reel seat on so he didn't have to strip down the rod completely. I figured I would try this one rod at a time, and if the first rod looked good, we could move on to the next rod or until I ran out of money.

Three or four weeks went by, and Dick finally showed up with the rewrapped spinning rod. The rod looked great, but he didn't have anywhere to epoxy the new wrapping. To make things a little more complicated, Dick ran out of thread. He stopped at Economy Tackle, picked up a few spools, and finished the butt section. It looked beautiful! The only problem was that the thread I bought had color preserver already applied, and the thread Dick bought didn't. The wrapping for the guides was bright, and the thread on the butt section was dull. It wasn't that big of a deal. When I took the rod to Economy Tackle, I made sure that the guy who was going to epoxy the rod knew enough to coat the butt section with a color preserver. Several days later, I stopped by to pick up my snook rod. I thought three days would be plenty of time for the epoxy to dry. I was standing at the counter talking to Mark, the owner's son, waiting for my rod.

When Ray Moss, the man working on my rod, came to the counter he was almost in tears. He showed me the rod. The wrapping on the butt section was dull, much duller than when I had dropped off the rod. Immediately, I knew what had happened. He forgot to put on the color preserver before he epoxied the butt section. Ray kept telling me he had no idea what happened. So I asked, "Did you put the color preserver on the thread before you epoxied the butt section?"

He put his hand on his head and apologized again. Ray kept telling me how sorry he was and that he would strip the rod and rewrap it. Then I asked him if he knew how to wrap quads and chevrons. Ray finally admitted he didn't.

Mark kept looking at me and finally asked me who wrapped the rod in the first place. At that point, I just gave up, grabbed the rod, and left. Mark followed me out the door, and we both cracked up laughing. I jumped in Mark's truck, and we went to Walt's Fish Market for lunch, where Mark painstakingly told me Ray Moss's life story.

Ray Moss was AKA Fertile Myrtle. We called him Fertile Myrtle because he had so many children, and he was far from calling it quits. Until a month before, Ray owned a sewing machine repair shop in Arcadia and, at the time, was going through a rough divorce. He lived in his father's old cracker house that was in disrepair and for the most part, worthless. But the property was worth a small fortune. Ray's father had built the house in the mid-fifties on a beautiful piece of property that butted the Ringling School of Art, which had been trying to buy the property for thirty years. Still, Ray's father refused to sell regardless of the offering price.

Ray is one of the nicest people you could ever meet, and he was very good at repairing fishing reels and just about everything else. A couple of weeks previously, Ray had stumbled into Economy Tackle looking for a job. Mark and his father hired him the next day before Ray could find another job. Ray also loved to fish, and better yet, he was an excellent fly fisherman and a fantastic fly tier. Ray wasn't in town for more than two weeks when he met a beautiful woman at the Five O'Clock Club, playing darts and downing a few beers. Not only was she good looking, but she was also very bright. They fell in love overnight, and several months later, they were married and immediately started having kids, as if Ray didn't have enough kids in Arcadia already. Often, I showed up in the middle of the night to go fishing and found Ray in the rocking chair with a baby in each arm.

The following week I was in Economy Tackle talking to Mark's sister when Ray walked up and apologized again. He was on his way to lunch and wanted to know if he could buy me lunch for screwing up my rod. We walked out the back door of Economy Tackle, where everyone kept their cars. We walked up to an old Florida Power and Light truck that had seen better days. It was orange in some spots, green in others. It had so much rust, I don't know how it could survive a speed bump without the fenders falling off. The doors creaked when you opened them. The windows were cracked in about five different places, and the passenger-side window was broken, stuck about three-quarters of the way open. It didn't have air conditioning, and the radio didn't work. The truck's bed had holes in it the size of five-gallon buckets. I asked Ray, "Where did you get this piece of junk?"

To hear Ray tell it, when FP&L finally gets finished with their work trucks, they auction them off a few times a year. So, I asked Ray, "How many miles does it have on the odometer?"

Ray pulled out the paperwork from the glove box. I opened the envelope and started reading. According to the mileage statement, the truck had 330,000+ miles on it when the odometer stopped working. Still, considering that the odometer hadn't worked for years, there was no telling just how many miles it recorded after it broke. I remember thinking, *that's all?* Then I looked at the auction receipt, and Ray had only paid $175 for this pile of rolling junk. Ray drove that pitiful-looking rust bucket around Sarasota for the next ten years before he finally bought a new Chevy truck.

Over lunch, Ray kept trying to bleed me for information about the local fishing, and I kept speaking in generalities. This wasn't my first rodeo, but then again, he was only one person. How much damage could one guy do? So, I offered him a few tidbits of information. First, I coughed up Humpback Bridge. I told him I always tried to catch the Humpback late at night on an outgoing tide. Ray pulled out a tide chart and started crossing out the bad tides, then he asked me if I wanted to fish it Thursday night. I said, "Sure, I will meet you up there around eleven o'clock at the beginning of the outgoing tide."

Ray said, "That works well. I have a fly-tying club meeting until nine o'clock."

I didn't think much about the fly-tying club at the time. However, when I had to meet someone on a particular bridge at a specific time, I always showed up early, and most of the time, I had already caught a few snook by the time my fishing buddy arrived. So, I decided to get there around nine or nine-thirty.

I loaded my bicycle around eight-thirty and headed for the Humpback. I turned the corner on Siesta Drive, and I couldn't believe my eyes! Fifteen or twenty cars must have been parked alongside the road. And right in the middle of all the new cars and trucks was Ray Moss's orange and green rust bucket. I tried to pull my bicycle up on the bridge and lean it against the railing, but there wasn't even room to walk, must less lean my bike. I remember walking up to Ray and screaming, "What are you doing and who are all these people?"

I think I yelled at him for the next twenty minutes. I was screaming so much that some of the fishermen went back to their cars. And after a few minutes, they started leaving. Ray told me they were the members of his fly-tying club, and they wanted to fish the Humpback with him. I was on the verge of getting violent. I learned a valuable lesson that night: Ray couldn't keep his mouth shut! When he learned about a hot fishing spot, he told everyone who walked through the front doors of Economy Tackle. I don't think it fazed him in the least. I still find it hard to believe that Ray and I became close friends for the next thirty years.

Summer was coming to an end much faster than I wanted. It was one of those confusing times when I had so many things going on in my life, and I had no idea how to finish any of them. School was about to start, I still had football practice every day, and Dick Clevenger was trying to teach me how to drive so I would be ahead of the curve when my driver's education class started.

The fall mullet run was in full swing, and Dick and the boys kept telling me about the incredible snook fishing during the winter months right behind Riverview High School. To hear Dick tell it, Phillippi Creek was stacked with snook as long as your leg throughout the winter. All I had to do was skip school, grab my rod, walk down to the creek, and then beat the snook off with a stick. It wasn't the first time I had heard about Phillippi Creek, and it wouldn't be the last. Dick was almost right about the snook.

We're Born, We Live,
We Die, on Our Terms

A few times a year, I managed to spend quality time with my father. He had transferred from Redstone Arsenal in Huntsville, Alabama, to NASA in Cape Canaveral. He wanted to be close to my Uncle John.

I have to be honest. I have no idea what my Uncle John did for a living. I'm not sure my Uncle John was my real uncle or my uncle in name only. My dad and uncle were die-hard baseball junkies. They played in multiple softball leagues several times a week, and they played in random semipro baseball leagues when they weren't playing softball. Both of them had played baseball at the University of Alabama. They were on baseball scholarships that didn't leave much money for food. So, they joined the National Guard to make a few extra bucks every month. Several months later, the Korean War broke out, and the army sent my father and my uncle to an out-of-the-way telecommunication station in Greenland for three years.

My father went into the army as a private, and three years later, he came out a private. When my father finally made it back to the University of Alabama, he changed his major from history to engineering. After graduation, he went to work for Redstone Arsenal.

Years later, I was in the navy stationed on Coronado in San Diego, California. But at that time, I was temporarily stationed in Japan at Yokosuka Naval Base for three months, and I received a phone call from the Veterans Administration in Tampa, Florida. My father had died earlier that day from cancer of the throat and cirrhosis of the liver. The Red Cross offered to fly me home for the funeral. I thought about it, but in the end, I passed and moved on. His situation was self-inflicted, and he knew what he was doing. It's tough to burn the candle at both ends and live to be an old man. In the end, I had a few beers and smiled. My father had lived life by his own rules.

He was forty-two years old when he died. He was an intelligent man, maybe too bright. He loved life, and I knew he loved me; that was something I was never sure about with my mother. I am not sure she was capable of loving anyone—especially herself.

School finally started, and eventually, football got underway. I had pep rallies to attend, cheerleaders to chase, and classes to sit through. For some reason, I didn't remember the old Fort Lauderdale High School as this organized, or maybe I should say, institutionalized. Then again, the old Fort Lauderdale High School was five times the size of Riverview High School. I didn't remember signing up for two study halls and drivers' education, but somehow that's what I got. If that wasn't strange enough, the study halls were back-to-back, and the teacher, or should I say class monitor, was the head football coach. I didn't get the chance to sit down before the coach came up to me and told me to get my butt down to the weight room and hit the weights. Odd, considering that study hall was held in the cafeteria, and the cafeteria was on the other side of the campus. Everyone from guidance counselors to hall monitors stopped me on the way to the weight room. Eventually, I stopped going to study hall and went directly to the gym.

And this was just the first day of school. This would be tough. It would take me years to adjust to this kind of institutional control.

· 25 ·

The Coastal Rivers and the Fertile Estuaries

$\mathcal{M}$y first semester at Riverview High School was troublesome. Some days I just wanted to pack my bags and fade away, as if school never existed. It wasn't easy to develop a rhythm, much less any consistency. Each day seemed to come replete with a new set of problems. For lack of a better explanation, like an Atlantic salmon, I was still swimming against the current. I was trying to do too many things at one time and, for the most part, not doing any of them very well. I needed to radically simplify my life, jettison the imaginary things holding me back, and rid myself of as many distractions as possible, then concentrate on the crucial task.

It sounded so easy. Of course, I wasn't getting any help at home, but that wasn't necessarily bad. The answers came from two very different people. For some reason, I found myself taking a general science course with Harold Maddox and an environmental conservation course with Dr. Tim Carnes. These two gentlemen were different in so many ways, yet they had so much in common.

Mr. Maddox was in his mid-thirties, a tall, slender man who rarely showed much emotion. He was a man of very few words. In some ways, Harold drove the kids crazy. When someone would ask him a question, he would respond in a "Paddy's answer," a mere rephrasing of the original question, anything but the solution. And yet, Harold never gave the impression that he didn't care. It was just the opposite. He would smile and work out the problem on the blackboard repeatedly until the light came on. He was one of the most patient teachers I can remember, and to make things a little more interesting, Harold loved to fish. Harold and his wife owned a twenty-five-foot Mako, rigged primarily to chase tarpon. But they also had

105

a garage full of canoes and wooden kayaks that they used for camping and exploring the backcountry.

Harold and his wife fished the multiple tarpon tournaments in Boca Grande every year. Once we had the chance to sit down and talk, my life seemed to get better instantly. I have no idea why. It could have been the fishing, or it could have been the stability in his life. He was never too high and never too low. It gave me a chance to relax and take a deep breath. Harold was certainly as laid back as they come; he was fascinated by anything and everything that had to do with fisheries, biology, and marine ecosystems. His wife, Sarah, a science teacher at Sarasota High School, volunteered for various environmental projects on the weekend and holidays and was always a little hyper when it came to details. But the woman loved to fish.

Sarah's motor never stopped, and if you got her started on one of her pet peeves, she could go on for hours. Sarah was the only person I had ever met at the time who could be in the middle of an argument, then walk away and weeks later remember precisely where she had been. Harold and Sarah were leftover hippies from the Haight-Ashbury days. They were hippies in every sense of the word. Sarah never stopped yapping about the Monterey Pop Festival and Woodstock. They were still firm believers in the counterculture ideas of the late sixties. It didn't seem that odd, considering that we were still in the early seventies.

Dr. Carnes was in his late sixties but still younger than any man half his age. The man had more energy than anyone I had ever met. At one time, he was one of the big shots in the U.S. Forestry Service. He was working his way up the ladder when he was involved in a horrific logging accident that cost him his right arm, but he never let the accident slow him down. Dr. Carnes had a booming voice and a great sense of humor. He was always making jokes about his missing arm. It took most kids a few days to get used to him, but in the end, I think he inspired more kids than any teacher I had ever met. It's a shame that didn't happen more often.

He knew more about logging and conservation than anyone I had ever known. I worked at Tall Timbers Research Station outside of Tallahassee when I was in graduate school. I spent a tremendous amount of time around people from the U.S. Forestry Service and the Nature Conservancy. I never met anyone who could have kept up with him. He had the kind of energy and enthusiasm rarely found in teachers. His office was constantly overrun with students. I don't remember him ever throwing anyone out. I think he liked me because I would listen to all his stories. Looking back, in some ways, he introduced me to the world I knew existed but until then I didn't know where the door in was.

The first time I hiked into the Lower Lake in Myakka State Park, I made the mistake of telling Dr. Carnes about it, and he made me write a report and read it to the class. I always thought it was corny, but Dr. Carnes knew exactly what he was doing.

Life can be funny at times. First, you're ready to walk away and live life on your terms. The next minute, you're skipping down the beach with a smile on your face, all because someone invited you to go fishing. Even though I spent as much time on the water, or more, as the average commercial fisherman, this was different. Harold and Sarah had invited me down to Charlotte Harbor for a few days of fishing. It was liberating to know that you could still get an excellent education, a beautiful wife, a wonderful home, and a twenty-five-foot Mako if your wife loved to fish. Best of all, you could spend your remaining days pursuing the things you love to do. You really could live life on your terms. It just involved a lot of work and finding the right spouse.

Until that point, my life had been a runaway locomotive on a very narrow track going pretty much nowhere except Siesta Key Bridge and O'Hara's Surf Shop. I derived what structure I had in my life at the time from people like Dick Clevenger and a guy named Wally. I loved them both, but I didn't want to end up like them. Until I met my wife thirty years ago, my life could have evolved in any direction. I could have spent my life living in a small apartment or a small travel trailer somewhere in the Florida Keys, working in a gas station, then spend the rest of the day on the water chasing bonefish or maybe the occasional permit. Who knows? Then for dinner, I could have feasted on the multitudes of mangrove snapper that called the bridges in the Florida Keys home, or if I was lucky, a chunky mutton snapper stuffed with shrimp and crabmeat. If nothing else, I could have pilfered the random lobster trap and dined on fresh Florida lobster and cheap wine every night. The daily mantra would have been to seize the day—carpe diem—to attack the day's efforts with vigor and purpose; squeeze the life out of every opportunity.

I had been dreaming about Charlotte Harbor for years. Christmas break couldn't come fast enough! My dreams overflowed with visions of stalking tailing redfish on the muddy grass flats of Bull Bay. I couldn't get the picture out of my head of a twenty-pound snook sucking down my fly on a skinny flat somewhere in Pine Island Sound. Wading a saltwater flat in the early morning on an incoming tide with a fly rod can be life changing. You have no idea what might come tailing over the edge. I have seen everything from tarpon to sharks testing the shallow waters, waiting for the opportunity to feed.

At this point, I was never going to make it until Christmas break. I had been thinking about Charlotte Harbor constantly for the past forty-eight hours. I didn't know much about the harbor. I knew where it was, and for the most part, I knew how to get there, but other than that, I was clueless. Then it hit me. If I could get Ralph to come over for a few days, we would have a flats boat and an offshore boat. All I had to do was get Ralph to answer his phone. It took four or five phone calls before I reached him that evening.

The life of a guide is anything but stable, especially for the good ones. It had been a while since we had last spoken. It was one of those situations where you wanted to call and catch up, but life always seemed to get in the way. We talked for what seemed like half the night. At that point, all I could think about was the long-distance phone bill. I had to spill my guts for the next hour. Ralph wanted to know everything about fishing on the west coast, right down to the smallest detail. He wanted to know about the snook, and he never shut up about the tarpon and the giant jewfish in Boca Grande Pass and someplace he called the phosphate docks. I barely had time to tell him that I hadn't had the chance to fish Boca Grande yet. That didn't stop him from filling in the details for me as if I were fishing the phosphate docks. Then, of course, I had to listen to endless stories about his new clients before I could get a word in edgewise about the Christmas break trip. I wanted to scream at the top of my lungs, "Give it a break! I have something I want to ask you."

But I didn't want to spoil his evening. Ralph was on a roll. All I could do was sit back and listen.

We talked about Brandon for what seemed like hours. Brandon was on his way to the University of Miami, and for some inexplicable reason, Ron had decided to join the navy. Then we both exploded and started to rant and rave about the population explosion working its way south and what it was doing to the fishing. Even though the development along the west coast was years behind the east coast, you could see the telltale signs of growth and development starting to creep in, not to mention the hordes of tourists that invaded South Florida during the season. It didn't take a rocket scientist to understand why the business community loved the tourist season. The massive traffic jams and long lines of tourists trying to get in and out of Walt's Fish Market and the Philippi Creek Oyster Bar every night were horrendous.

It was only a matter of time before the fishing in South Florida would go the way of the dodo bird. At the time, I didn't know how bad it could get. I finally told him about Harold and Sarah and the fishing trip. Ralph wanted to fish in Charlotte Harbor, and I thought this would be a perfect opportunity. Even better, Brandon should be home for Christmas break. I could hear the gears grinding in Ralph's head through the phone lines, and in the background, I could hear Linda looking for his spiral notebook where she kept his customers' personal information. The next thing I knew, Linda was on the phone, and even before we shared a few pleasantries, she screamed, "Can I go?"

All I could say was, "Sure. Why not?"

At this point, I had to be careful about explaining Ralph to Harold and Sarah. I knew that Linda and Sarah would get along great, but Ralph and Harold were a different story. It was almost impossible to get Ralph to stop playing guide and just fish like a normal fisherman. It wasn't in his DNA. I knew that if Ralph had an idea, it wouldn't be simple. The problem was that Ralph was master and commander of his flats boat, and when you were on his skiff, you did as Ralph told you to do. I never found that to be a problem, but I was a teenager, and they were all adults. And from what little I knew about adults at the time, they rarely played well together.

It was Friday night, and I knew Dick wanted to fish that night, but I needed to get a good night's sleep. So, I called "Mother" and told her to let Dick know I wouldn't to be able to make it and that I would explain everything Saturday night. I called Harold to make sure that he and Sarah would be home the next day. Sarah invited me over for breakfast Saturday morning, something about pancakes and bacon.

Harold wanted me to stop by Ricky's house and beg, borrow, or steal a bottle of cane syrup from his mother. Ricky's mom and dad were both dyed-in-the-wool Florida crackers. Earlier that year, Ricky's mom had invited me in for homemade buttermilk biscuits, churned butter, and freshly milled cane syrup. I kept telling Harold and Sarah about it, and I kept getting invited over for breakfast; all I had to do was supply the cane syrup. I tried my best to explain to Sarah about the scrambled eggs and mullet roe Ricky's mother kept serving us for dinner. Sarah turned up her nose and politely left the room, as if I had offended her highfalutin taste buds.

Who knew that all it took to offend a highly educated, easy-going hippie was a plate of scrambled eggs and mullet roe. On the other hand, Harold started salivating. It was heavenly. I remember it like it was yesterday: scrambled eggs and mullet roe, a side of smoked mullet, cheese grits, and iced tea—and if you were lucky, a bowl of homemade banana ice cream made in an old-fashioned wooden ice cream churn. I always volunteered to churn the ice cream because I loved to stick my finger in the drain hole and lick the salt off my fingers.

I managed to get two Mason jars of cane syrup from Ricky's mom. She wanted to know what I was doing with all of it, and I confessed that I was using some of it to bribe Harold and Sarah, so I might get a better grade in Harold's class, if nothing else.

It was time to ease my way into a conversation about Ralph and Linda.

All I had to do was get to Harold's house without breaking the Mason jars. It was a short bike ride. They lived on Midnight Pass Road a few blocks south of Stickney Point Road. I pulled up in the driveway, and I could smell the bacon cooking. About halfway through breakfast, I started talking about the fishing trip.

I started by telling Sarah about Linda and how much they had in common. Fundamentally, they were the same person. They shared the same likes and dislikes, and they were both children of the sixties. Sarah asked what she did for a living and where she lived, all sorts of small talk. Then I casually mentioned to Harold that her husband was one of the top guides on the east coast. Ralph had a great flats boat, and he guided about 250 days a year. Out of the blue, Harold mentioned, "It's a shame that they live on the east coast. I would love to meet these guys."

I replied, "I know they like to take a few weeks off over Christmas—maybe I can get Ralph to drag his flats boat over for a few days and fish with us. It might be nice to have two boats, especially if one was a flats boat."

Sarah immediately responded, "That would be awesome."

I kept thinking, *OK, what just happened?* Could it be that easy? But, of course, at this juncture, I couldn't take credit for anything without admitting that I had invited Ralph and Linda without telling Harold and Sarah.

After breakfast, Harold put my bicycle in the back of his truck and gave me a ride home. I barely had a chance to walk through the door before my mother told me that Ralph had called several times. I didn't want to call him back because I would be on the hook for another phone bill. I still had no idea what I would tell my parents when the first phone bill came. I had barely started to clean and stack my surfboards when my mother screamed, "Ralph's on the phone."

I hoped this would be quick. Peter was on his way over to help me take my surfboards to the shop; I was going to rack them in the back room with all of their surfboards. I picked up the phone. Before I even had the chance to say "hi," Ralph jumped in and immediately started describing his grand plan. I could hear Linda in the background filling in the pieces Ralph was leaving out that she obviously thought were important.

From what I made of the conversation, Ralph had an extremely wealthy customer who owned a six-bedroom home with a pool on the water on Captiva Island. The owners always celebrated Christmas in Minnesota with their family and friends and never came down until a few days after the New Year. It was a big property—so big the caretaker lived on it, and the chef and cleaning staff were on call 365 days a year. The home had an enormous dock and came equipped with two flats boats and a twenty-seven-foot Morgan. If Ralph didn't want to deal with his boat, he had free run of the property and the other boats. The fishing trip was starting to sound too good to be true, but I knew Ralph had a few very wealthy customers. At this point, I thought it was time to hook up Ralph and Linda with Harold and Sarah and let them get to know each other and work out the details.

Days went by, and I hadn't heard about the trip. I tried to ask Harold about it in class, but he told me to "hang in there."

I could only assume that things were going well. Other than putting together the four of them, I contributed very little to the operation. Toward the end of the week, Harold invited me over for breakfast Sunday morning. After a quick breakfast, Sarah cleared the table and started laying out maps and various charts of Charlotte Harbor. She had already begun highlighting the deep channels and the shallow grass flats from Gasparilla Pass in the north to the mangrove-covered islands that dominated the landscape throughout Pine Island Sound to the south. There were so many moving parts. I looked over at Harold and just started laughing. Sarah was in the zone, and I don't think you could have slowed her down if you wanted to. The maps and charts were nothing more than a chessboard to Sarah.

She used fluorescent green markers to highlight places they had fished before and yellow fluorescent markers to highlight the areas she wanted to fish this time. And when Sarah broke out the protractor and compass, I just sighed. When she opened her briefcase and pulled out a slide rule, I almost fell off the chair. It was beginning to look more like an amphibious assault than a fishing trip. Sarah kept talking about contingency plans. I finally chimed in, "What do contingency plans mean?"

Then she talked about cold fronts, two tide days, one tide days, red tide, green algae, blue algae, dinoflagellates, and finally, diatoms. Then she told me to stop cursing. I shrugged my shoulders and looked at Harold again, and all he could say was, "I told you to pay attention in class."

The only thing I could come up with at the time was, "It's a good thing we don't have to pay for this trip."

Of course, I knew that was a canard of sorts—there is no such thing as a free trip. Knowing Ralph and Linda, I could only assume they were doing the same thing. Then Sarah gave me even better news. Ralph managed to get the house from Christmas Eve through January second. The good news just kept coming. We managed to get full access to the housekeeping staff, and the owner was letting everyone stay there for free as a Christmas present for Ralph and Linda. It would be a little over two months before we packed up and headed south to Captiva Island.

I couldn't imagine waiting two more months! Somehow, I needed to figure out how to get my sixteen-foot aluminum canoe down there. I asked Harold and Sarah if they wanted to take a few exploratory trips in the canoes and kayaks. After all, we had the weekends, and we still had a long weekend for Thanksgiving. We had the entire week before Christmas to do some reconnaissance. Sarah pulled out the tide charts and started picking dates. She didn't know if the weekends would work because of all her obligations, but she thought we could spend a few days on Sanibel over Thanksgiving.

At that point, I needed to find someone who was old enough to have reliable transportation, the weekends off, and liked to fly-fish. That left Dick off the list; his car was a piece of junk. I don't think Dick had ever waded in his life, and Wally was way too big to fit in a canoe, and Lou's wife would have shot down the trip before he even got started. The only person I could think of was Ray Moss, and Ray did have transportation. The question was, would his truck make it to Charlotte Harbor and back?

Paddle Like Heck and Hope for the Best

*L*ater that night, I called Ray and tried to explain the ins and outs of my plan. If nothing else, I wanted to work my way south on the weekend and fish the flats, creeks, beaches, and the backcountry down to Charlotte Harbor. We could cherry-pick our way down and only fish the places that looked productive. The problem was that, like the Everglades, it all looked productive. I decided to buy a journal and try to keep quality notes. I wanted to record the location, the tides, the weather, and the number and species of fish. I think Sarah was wearing off on me. Ray never said much on the phone; for the most part, I always thought I was talking to myself.

Ray thought about it for a few days and finally capitulated. We had to develop a plan, so we decided to start small and stay relatively close to home. Saturday morning, we put in at Midnight Pass and used the incoming tide to float into Little Sarasota Bay, wade the grass flats, and later float out on the outgoing tide. We wouldn't have to paddle or pole much if it worked. If we were lucky, the tides and the wind would do all the work for us.

Saturday morning finally reared its ugly head. Life can be a paradox at times. You dream of getting up early to go fishing, you roll over and finally find the alarm clock, then knock it on the floor, which means you have to get up, drag yourself into the kitchen, and put on the coffee pot. Then it finally dawns on you: this sucks! Ray picked me up around four-thirty so we could stop at the Ranch House for breakfast. The tide didn't change for a few more hours. After breakfast, we could pitch plugs for snook on the Stickney Point Bridge. However, it never happened. We sat around drinking coffee and lost all track of time. By the time we realized what time it was, the tide was starting to flood.

We put in the canoe at the public boat ramp at Turtle Beach, loaded our gear, and pushed off. The boat ramp was right around the corner from Midnight Pass, and it only took us minutes to get there. We hugged the mangrove shoreline to eliminate some of the drag on the canoe. The tide was strong, and it was pushing a lot of water.

We probably should have shown up at the boat ramp a half hour earlier. When we managed to get to the pass, the sun was starting to come up in the east. It was a beautiful morning, even with the black and purple thunderheads in the south. The day was full of early-morning promise. At that point, we paddled out into the current and started drifting south. I stood up in the canoe and grabbed the push pole to steer the canoe. Ray stood up in the front and started stripping line off his fly reel. Once he had sixty or seventy feet of fly line lying in the bottom of the canoe, he made a few false casts, then stripped his line in, stacking the fly line from bottom to top in case he saw some jacks busting bait or some rolling tarpon.

We drifted south for about seven or eight miles, following the mangrove shorelines that buffered the backside of Casey Key. We spent the entire day on the west side of the bay, pounding the tiny mangrove islands and oyster bars that protected the multitude of million-dollar homes from the occasional storm surge. I don't think we stepped out of the canoe once except to eat lunch on an old dock attached to an empty lot. The weather passed quickly, and the remainder of the day was tourist fodder for the local Chamber of Commerce. Temperatures stayed in the mid-seventies even through the hottest part of the day.

The humidity, the bane of everyone's lifestyle in South Florida, was almost nonexistent, with or without the threat of thunderstorms. We didn't catch any big fish that day, but we did manage to find and catch a potpourri of almost everything. It seemed like every pothole we came to managed to provide a few juvenile redfish or trout, and the majority of the docks we fished were stacked with small snook and an endless supply of the poor man's tarpon, aka ladyfish.

We finally reached a point of no return. Casey Key was bound to the north by Midnight Pass and bound to the south by the Venice Inlet. About midway from either pass, you reach a dilemma. The tide was coming in or out in two different directions simultaneously. If you wanted to come out the same way you went in, you had to stop and turn around before you got caught in the current going in the opposite direction. Of course, that only applies to canoes because of the lack of propulsion. Then again, you could paddle like heck and hope for the best. I can only assume that the Calusa Indians had this figured out ten or twelve thousand years ago; then again, we have no way of knowing what the terrain looked like then.

Like clockwork, every Saturday and Sunday, we ventured a little farther south for the next month. We never made it to Charlotte Harbor because we explored so much along the way, but we did manage to find some great fishing spots. Unfortunately, the year was getting a little short in the tooth, the water temperature was dropping, and the fish were on the move. It was the time of the harvest moon—a time to fatten up for the leaner times ahead.

Thanksgiving on Sanibel Island

$\mathcal{A}$t some point, you have to come to terms with the fact that you're fifteen years old, and no matter how mature you act, and no matter how much you think you know, adults will still treat you like a fifteen-year-old. I will freely admit that I couldn't cast a fly rod like Ted Williams, I couldn't tie a fly like Lefty Kreh, and I couldn't pole a flats boat like Flip Pallot; and no, I hadn't traveled the world like A. J. McClane. But I would be willing to bet hard cash that I had spent as much time on the water by the age of fifteen as any one of them.

I know this will probably offend some people, but fishing on the east coast and the Florida Keys is not the same as fishing on the west coast. I am not saying one side of the state of Florida is better than the other. I am saying it was different. The attitudes of the fishermen were utterly different. It was night and day. On the east coast, they lived to fish. I knew fishermen who would push a shopping cart out on the pier with thirty or forty rods and stay, not for the night, but for the week.

Their wives and kids would bring dinner to them in the evening, then stay for a few hours, go home, and return the following evening and do the same thing. Granted, many of these guys probably were unemployed. However, most were die-hard fishermen who were passionate about their chosen lifestyle. They were incredibly nice people to be around but very difficult to understand.

When an adult tells you that we're going to Charlotte Harbor for the next three days, I immediately think that means we are going fishing for the next three days. Another thing I noticed about adults was that they never altogether told a lie, but they lived on the razor's edge, close enough to traverse both sides of the blade and at the same time deny all culpability.

The only reason I could make this trip in the first place was that I had ruptured my appendix three weeks earlier. The doctor told me I was finished with football for the year, so I did what any fifteen-year-old kid would do. I went back to practice six days later and lied to the head coach.

That's the difference between kids and adults. I blatantly lied, and I admit it. I told him I was cleared to play, and on the third play, my stitches broke, and I started bleeding through my jersey. The team doctor came over, lifted my jersey, and when he saw the damage, he went ballistic. I think they overreacted when they saw the blood. I was done for the season, but I wasn't in any pain, and if they had calmed down long enough and thought the process through, I could have finished out the season. Instead, I went fishing.

We tried to get out of town early on the twenty-fourth to avoid the Thanksgiving traffic. Harold and Sarah pulled up in front of my house around two o'clock that afternoon. I had my gear packed and stacked on the porch. I knew better than to overdo it this time, so I only packed three or four spinning rods, a fly rod, a bag full of clothes, and a small tackle bag. I figured they had everything else we might need for a three-day fishing trip.

Harold had managed to rent a small house on Sanibel just west of the lighthouse. That was pretty much considered a coup over Thanksgiving. Thanksgiving now seems nothing more than a prelude to Christmas. From what I remember, more people appeared to celebrate the holiday season with their families when I was growing up.

The house was reasonably close to the marina where Harold would tie up the boat. The marina was on the mainland side of the causeway and seemed easy enough to get to in the mornings. When Harold finally pulled up, I noticed two other cars pull in behind. Harold had invited his mother and father, and Sarah had invited her sister and two kids down for Thanksgiving. I wasn't quite sure what that meant, but that brought the number of people occupying that small house to eight.

Harold helped load my gear into the Suburban, and he never said one word about his mother and father, much less Sarah's sister and her kids. I found that vaguely revealing. Either he didn't think it was any of my business, or he didn't think it was necessary. Fair enough: I wasn't going to back out at the last moment. Who knows? I might never get invited again. I kept thinking about Ralph and Linda; that was a different story altogether. At the moment, there was absolutely nothing I could do except enjoy the next three days and cross that bridge when I got to it.

We barely made it over the Stickney Point Bridge before pulling into the Gulf Gate Shopping Center. It seemed we were about to stock up for Thanksgiving dinner. The problem was that everybody else in Sarasota had the same idea. Publix was a zoo! Twenty or thirty people must have been in each line, waiting to check out. I was biting my lip. Somehow, I had been left off the planning committee altogether. I didn't know if I had to buy my food, or if they would take care of everything. I gingerly asked Harold, "What's up? What do I need to pick up?"

He just smiled and told me to "push the cart. We got it; we will be out of here in no time at all."

With a deep sigh of relief, I just pushed the cart. They were buying enough food to feed Patton's Third Army, which was apropos because we were starting to resemble Patton's Third Army.

Forty-five minutes later, we were finally heading south. The roads were worse than I thought they would be. It seemed like everyone was headed south to visit someone for the holidays. It was a long drive. We probably would not make Sanibel before nightfall. That meant we wouldn't be able to put the boat in the water until Thanksgiving morning. I was about to ask, "Did anyone check with the marina to make sure they were going to be open on Thanksgiving?"

Then again, I didn't want to insult anyone on the first day. After all, I was just a fifteen-year-old kid, right?

I assumed they probably thought that was above my pay grade. My expectations were going south faster than the Suburban. Little did I know at the time, but Harold had prepaid the marina for the slip, and the security guard would let us in. Harold backed the trailer down a few feet, and Sarah unclipped the straps and disconnected the winch. Then Harold backed the trailer down into the water until the Mako began to float. Sarah grabbed the rope attached to the forward and aft cleats and steadied the boat while Harold pulled the Suburban back up to the parking lot. Considering that it was a twenty-five-foot Mako, a substantial center console by nature, it came off with the skill and precision of a high-school science project.

So far, it had been a long day, and the lack of food and sleep would irritate anyone. But at least we were on Sanibel Island and supposedly headed in the right direction. We made a left turn on Periwinkle, and after what seemed like a mile or so, we made another left on Buttonwood Lane. We were looking for a small white house with blue trim on the right-hand side of the road. When Harold finally located the house, he parked along the street in the front yard. My first impression of the tiny house was, "Yep; it's a small house."

About that time, Harold's mother and father pulled into the driveway, and a minute or two later, Sarah's sister and two kids. Harold opened the front door and took a deep breath. Fortunately, it had four bedrooms, and I'm giving the owners the benefit of the doubt. It was more like one main bedroom, two smaller bedrooms, and one rather large walk-in closet. I didn't have to ask which one was mine. I started unloading my fishing gear and clothes into the smallest bedroom, more suitably fitted for Bilbo Baggins. It took hours to unload all the food and put it away.

At about that time, Sarah realized that we needed to eat something. Everyone was beginning to get a little grumpy. The temperature was rising in the house, even though the air conditioner's thermostat read sixty-five degrees. Harold grabbed my shoulder and asked me if I wanted to go with him and scrounge up something for dinner. I jumped at the opportunity to get away from Sarah's two nephews. We managed to find a grocery store at the other end of the island—Bailey's General Store. It was a great little market. It had anything you could have possibly wanted, including homemade pies, fresh bread, and produce so ripe you could smell it the minute you walked through the front door.

The seafood department was exceptional! The fishmonger's display case was full of whole fish stacked like cordwood and smothered in crushed ice. In addition, it held fresh grouper, whole snapper, and an incredible member of the grouper family called a scamp. Fresh jumbo shrimp were in another display case, loads of smoked mullet fillets, and the crème de la crème, fresh stone crab claws in various sizes. The fish were so fresh that the seafood department didn't smell like fish. It didn't take a genius to see that Bailey's worked closely with the local commercial fishermen.

We loaded up on fresh loaves of homemade bread and a few pies, including a pecan pie from the bakery, and an assortment of cheeses and fresh meats from the deli, and a few quarts of smoked mullet dip. I tried to convince Harold to pick up a few pounds of fresh shrimp and a couple of pounds of stone crab claws, but he wasn't having any part of it. I think he was afraid of what Sarah might say or what Sarah might do. Finally, it seemed to me, we were long past the point of no return. We feasted that night for what seemed like hours. I was beginning to appreciate Sarah and her mother—not only did they love to cook, but with her sister's help, they put away the food and finished the dishes.

Then again, in a few hours, it would be Thanksgiving. Soon the tiny house would be awash in the scents of roasted turkey, homemade cornbread dressing, giblet gravy, and Harold's mother's famous string bean casserole. I didn't have the heart to tell her I hated string beans. Instead, Harold and I teamed up to make our first low-country boil and the pièce de résistance, pecan pie à la mode. Thanksgiving dinner was scheduled for five o'clock the next day. It was difficult to understand anyone that night—everyone was talking over each other. From the sound of the blended conversations, everyone but me wanted to sleep in the following day. I wanted to go fishing.

Of course, I didn't have any transportation except the shoes on my feet, but I was only several hundred yards from the water. On the nightstand was an old radio alarm clock. I didn't know whether it worked, much less how to set the alarm. So, I asked Harold to come see if he knew how to set the alarm. That solved two problems. This way, Harold would realize I wanted to get up early and fish in the morning instead of sleeping in, and second, have him show me how to set the alarm clock. When he asked what time I wanted to set the clock for, I told him five a.m.

He just smiled. "Good luck."

I was already awake when the alarm went off. It was still dark outside, so I left my fishing gear on the porch, made myself a coffee, and then started walking down to the end of the street. At the time, a public path wound its way between a few docks and piles of broken limestone down to the water. The sun was starting to show itself. The intense heat and humidity had left Sanibel months ago. From where I was sitting, it would be a beautiful sunrise.

At that time, Sanibel was growing, but it still had the look and feel of a small village. Access to the beaches was still abundant. For the most part, you could walk as far as you wanted to go in any direction. I remember sitting on a rough piece of old limestone that probably had been quarried almost a hundred years ago, long before the state built the lighthouse in 1884. I was enjoying the view and savoring my cup of coffee.

Then out of nowhere, the beach exploded! It looked like fish were every-where. From what I could see in the dim light, they were primarily big jacks, but other species had to be in on the blitz; I could only assume snook were somewhere, maybe even mackerel. Probably dozens of different species were in and around and beneath the school of bait. The light was still too dim to tell what kind of bait was getting crushed. Then a school of jacks chased a handful of pilchards up on the beach. The pilchards only lasted for several seconds before the birds devoured them.

The tide was ripping, and everything was alive. The pelicans moved in and started snapping at any bait near the surface. The seagulls squawked and screeched in disapproval as they tried to steal the pilchards from the pelicans. Great blue herons, little blue herons, and snowy egrets were in the shallow water, dozens of other shorebirds were running up and down the beach, and my rods were back on the porch. I kept sitting there for the next half hour or so, enjoying my cup of coffee. I was fascinated by the show playing out in front of me.

It was a game of life and death, which repeated itself more than a million, maybe billions of times a day. For some reason, I thought I was supposed to be there at that very moment. It just felt right. At some point in life, you come to the conclusion that in order to live life, you have to participate. As much as I loved to fish, and make no mistake about it, I lived to fish, but at the same time, I had always taken the time to enjoy nature, even at the most primal level.

Fishing is nothing more than a game to be played. It's not a sport, and it's not a competition. However, I will admit that I have enjoyed the competition in certain situations. On the other hand, surfing gave me that tactile connection with nature that you can't get from fishing. If you fall off your surfboard in the wrong place, at the wrong time, you might get to see the world from a pilchard's perspective.

Years later, I was fishing the bridge that crosses over Gasparilla Pass at the northern end of Charlotte Harbor. I was jigging for pompano with two of my closest friends, Mark Riehemann and Walt Winton. Mark and I had caught the same number of pompano. At the top of the tide, the best part of the tide, Mark wanted to go have lunch. I wouldn't leave without being what we used to call "high hook."

Primarily, it refers to the person who caught the most fish that day. Then again, it could refer to the largest fish caught that day. The rules should be defined as early as possible. And yes, I caught another pompano before we left. It seemed like an innocent game to play, but it was anything but innocent—it was downright ruthless at times, though in a friendly sort of way. Mark didn't have a competitive bone in his body. On the other hand, I couldn't leave without catching another fish. In the grand scheme of things, we are who we are, regardless of who we want to be.

Eventually, I made it back to the house to grab my fishing gear and started exploring. I wanted to head east, see the lighthouse, and fish the point, especially because the tide had changed. Finally, the sun was up, and the beaches were stunning. The water was as clear as any water I had ever seen. It reminded me of the Florida Keys. I was amazed at all the grass flats on the island's north side. Everywhere I looked, the backside seemed to be knee-deep in turtle grass and oyster beds. You could float the grass flats for days and never run out of places to fish. Ralph and Brandon were going to have a blast over Christmas.

· 28 ·

Life Is All about Timing

$\mathcal{D}$epending upon your location, it wasn't easy to describe exactly where you were on Sanibel, so much so that the people who lived on Sanibel didn't even understand it half the time. The barrier islands that follow the coast south traditionally run north and south. On the other hand, Sanibel runs east and west for the most part. It's only relevant if the winds were blowing out of the southwest, and you were determined to get out of the wind.

I didn't want to carry a lot of gear, so I grabbed one spinning rod and threw a small bag over my shoulder containing a few plugs, bucktails, and spare leader material. It was a day better suited for exploration, not necessarily fishing. That's not to say that I wouldn't fish, given the opportunity. If I ran into another blitz like the one that I had experienced this morning, I couldn't stop myself. Walking down the beach that morning, I fell in love with Sanibel. The white, sandy beaches were almost too pristine to believe; even on the island's backside, the beaches stretched for miles. Birds were feasting on the enormous schools of pilchards, and if you looked close enough, you could make out giant boils on the water's surface. If you take the time to study the different types of bait, you begin to realize that almost every predator has a distinct fingerprint. Some crash the bait on the surface, like big jacks; others, mackerel and kingfish, slice through the schools of bait; and still others, such as snook, prefer to feed closer to the bottom, at least the larger ones. Of course, there are a thousand variations on the theme.

At times, the morning seemed to stand still; there was so much to take in. The taste, the smells, and the sounds were occasionally overwhelming. I could only imagine what the rest of Charlotte Harbor was like, and if it was anything like Sanibel, I had found a new home. Over the next several hours, I walked north on the front side. Schools of bait stretched along the beach as far as you could see. I could only imagine the number of snook lying underneath them. What I didn't see much of was people—then again, the island didn't seem very crowded, considering that it was Thanksgiving.

Eventually, the tide started to slow down. It was only a matter of time before the current changed directions. By this time, I had made my way back to the lighthouse. When the tide finally stopped, I was standing in waist-deep water, working a large bucktail. I was trying to decide if I wanted to fish the first hour of the outgoing tide or go back to the house and take a nap. The first hour of the tide change can be cosmic.

Fishing is all about timing. I wanted to be in good spirits for dinner. At about that time, the tide changed direction, and I was almost swept away by the current. The water hit me like a small brick wall. I wasn't in danger of being washed out to sea because the tide wasn't strong enough to do any damage; the tide differential that day was only about a foot and a half. I kept thinking about the books I had read lately about the great Northwest and the giant tidal swings in some of the river mouths, especially the Columbia River. I could only imagine what a ten- or twelve-foot tide differential could do to you if you were in the wrong place at the wrong time. Deep down inside, I knew I was bound for Oregon and Washington; Pacific steelhead kept calling my name. At the time, I didn't know when or even how I would get there. I reeled in my bucktail and headed back to the house.

Thanksgiving dinners are always fun if nothing else. I knew the roasted turkey and dressing would be great by the aromas floating out of the kitchen. I knew I was in good hands when I saw the baked macaroni and cheese come out of the oven. After dinner, I planned to pig out on pecan pie and vanilla ice cream, then crawl between the covers for the next twenty-four hours. The only problem I could foresee at the time was Sarah's two nephews. We only had one giant turkey, and unless this turkey had three legs, somebody would get shortchanged. I figured I was probably the only one thinking about this, and maybe, I should show some restraint, take the high road, and leave the drumsticks for the kids. After all, I was nothing more than a freeloader masquerading as a guest, although for the most part, we were on Sanibel, thanks to me.

Harold pretty much gave up on the low-country boil. We still had two days left to put one together, but we already had so much food, and for the most part, we didn't think anybody would miss it. Harold's mother and father were headed to Marathon the following day to spend time with Harold's sister. Sarah's sister and her two nephews were going to head home sometime Saturday morning. That meant I was on my own again Friday. I thought I would work my way down to the causeway and check out the fishing on the Sanibel side.

It had been a long time since I participated in an authentic Thanksgiving dinner. It felt good. Who knew when the next time might be? Unfortunately, my mother and stepfather's idea of Thanksgiving dinner never amounted to much. More often than not, we ended up at some bland run-of-the-mill restaurant. The most memorable Thanksgiving dinner we had was when my stepfather brought home a few pizzas from Pizza Hut. It was one of the best Thanksgiving dinners I have ever eaten.

It was pretty much like I had anticipated. The kids grabbed the two drumsticks, and I was left with the thighs and some breast meat. I was laughing, but I don't think anyone knew why. It didn't matter because the giblet gravy was excellent! I could have grabbed the fresh rolls, stolen the gravy boat, floated away, and never looked back. Instead, I kept thinking, *Don't forget the pecan pie and vanilla ice cream.* A few hours later, the night pretty much faded. Everyone was stuffed, and the ladies were wading through the mess in the kitchen.

The following day came fast. I could have slept for another hour and still fished the same tide if I had wanted to. If the tides are constant from day to day, they usually run anywhere from forty-five minutes to an hour later the following day. So, if the tides change at seven in the morning on Monday, they will change around eight o'clock Tuesday morning. It also depends upon whether you have a four-tide day or a two-tide day. From my experience, two-tide days could be tough to fish.

Fortunately, we had four-tide days for the next five or six days, and I wanted to catch another sunrise. Unfortunately, when I finally made it down to the causeway, I ran into several problems. First, the bridge had no sidewalks, and the places I wanted to fish were between the two bridges. Signs everywhere said the bridge was off-limits to pedestrians. I had to think about that one for a moment. I could only assume that I was a pedestrian.

Who in his right mind would build a bridge that you couldn't walk across, much less fish? Then again, signs were everywhere you looked on Sanibel, informing people what they could and could not do. It must have been the idea of some alien brainchild from the Northeast. To this day, Sanibel has more rules and regulations than any place I have ever had the pleasure to fish. I was only fifteen years old, but I knew at some fundamental level that I was getting screwed.

Little did I know at the time, it was only the beginning. I had two choices, and neither sounded appealing. I could either stay on the backside and wade the grass flats west of the bridge or find a way to the front side without backtracking to the lighthouse. The tide was starting to rip, so I decided to stay on the backside until lunch and see what happened.

I waded in up to my knees and started pitching a Zara Spook as far as I could. I started ripping it back over the surface of the grass and then stopped it. Then I walked it for ten or twelve feet, let it sit there for a few seconds, and then started all over. I know it doesn't sound easy, but it's not that difficult. On my second cast something crushed my Zara Spook and started digging for the bottom!

I thought I had hooked a massive redfish. I tugged for what seemed like twenty minutes. Eventually, I pulled in a giant ball of grass, in the middle of which was a two- or three-pound redfish. If I could have weighed the grass and the redfish together, I would have had something in the twenty-pound range. I caught a few redfish and dozens of sea trout over the next several hours—nothing very big, but the sea trout averaged three, maybe four pounds. I hadn't seen many sea trout that large south of the Indian River.

The best part of the day was wading all the grass flats, and the worst part of the day was fishing those same flats. The higher the tide, the better the fishing, and the less I got snagged. Right before I quit fishing, I had several shots at monster jacks that looked like they were pushing twenty-five pounds. I did everything I could to get them to take, but all they wanted to do was play.

When I started walking back to the house, the water was several feet over the grass. I always thought the top of the tide was better than the bottom. It's been my experience that the more water in the bay, the better your chances are of catching something—the fish don't seem to be as nervous.

I got back just in time to catch Harold loading his fishing gear in the back of the Suburban. Come to find out, he was on his way to find me. Harold wanted to take the boat out for a while. He didn't have to twist my arm, but I did first run into the house and grab had a few leftovers. I was hungry, and no telling how long we would be out. I grabbed a turkey sandwich, some dressing, and a piece of pecan pie. It disappeared before we got to the marina. We parked the Suburban, and I started loading the fishing gear into the boat. I asked Harold where we were heading.

He replied, "I think we are going to hit the beaches and work our way down to Boca Grande and then fish our way back."

The tide was just starting to rip when we pulled out of the marina and circled the lighthouse. I didn't have any idea where we were going. I had a light spinning rod with a Penn 710 spooled with twelve-pound test, which seemed like a toy in a boat this big.

I asked Harold about the phosphate docks and what was special about them. Every person I ran into on the west coast knew about the phosphate docks. They were one step short of the Holy Grail of fishing. I half expected Saint Peter, the patron saint of fishermen, to be standing on the end of the docks, blessing the fishing boats as they floated by within shouting distance. At least today, I might get to see them, and better yet, I might get to fish them.

It felt good to be on the water. The Mako made the run down to Boca Grande in about twenty minutes. The ocean was as flat as a pancake. We turned into the Boca Grande channel and slowed down. It was amazing how much water was pouring out of Boca Grande Pass that day; in some ways, it reminded me of Port Everglades on steroids. It was three times the size of Sebastian Inlet and twice as powerful. Harold had to leave the boat in gear so he didn't lose ground against the current.

For some reason, I thought Harold was looking for something. He kept turning his head fore and aft. The only thing that caught my eye was the gas dock. Then off in the distance, I saw a broken-down pier with ratty old conveyer belts swinging in all directions. As we started to turn the corner, I got a better look at what I could only assume were the phosphate docks. I don't want to say it was a little anticlimactic, but I couldn't believe this dilapidated pile of lumber was the Holy Grail everybody kept describing. But, of course, it didn't matter what the docks looked like. What mattered was what was under them.

Harold eventually made his way across the pass to the backside of Cayo Costa. He pulled the Mako reasonably close to the mangroves, put the motor in neutral, and floated out with the tide. Large passes such as Boca Grande tend to have a varied landscape. For the most part, the mouth usually is made up of shifting shorelines and a combination of finely crushed sand and broken seashells. Usually, the deeper the pass, the more stable it is. Unfortunately, the Army Corps of Engineers did its best to screw up every pass in the state so they didn't have to dredge them several times a year. As a result, seawalls and jetties now constrict most of Florida's waterways. Boca Grande Pass was lucky; it was still pristine in so many ways. The landscape was still intact.

Charlotte Harbor, a massive estuary, was really an amalgamation of smaller estuaries and river mouths. The river mouths were smothered in thick organic muck and oyster bars, and the shorelines were choked with red mangroves. At low tide, the mudflats and oyster bars teemed with birds feeding on the tiny crustaceans—fiddler crabs and the multitude of other small bivalves that live in the brackish rivers and bays of Charlotte Harbor.

Harold was scouting the giant mangroves that jutted out from the shoreline, especially ones that had deep undercut banks caused by the wear and tear of enormous tides and twisting currents. If conditions were right and the water was clear, it was like looking into a saltwater aquarium. Sandbars and oyster beds funneled the water in various directions; coupled with the stability of the mangroves, they created nooks and crannies for the fish to travel in and search for food.

I thought Harold was looking for snook, but he wasn't. Instead, he was looking for small jewfish, if there was such a critter. I kept looking at my light spinning rod, thinking it had better be a very small jewfish. We floated with the current for another ten minutes, and before we reached the mouth of the pass, Harold decided to head inside and start fishing our way back to the marina. The tide was dropping fast.

• 29 •

There and Back Again

We worked our way back from Boca Grande Pass and fished a few flats that looked promising but without much to show for our effort. The problem was the Mako. A twenty-five-foot boat is not exactly a flats boat. It draws a considerable amount of water, which, for the most part, limits you to the deeper flats. Even if you wanted to anchor the boat and fish the skinny water, you had to climb out of the boat. The gunwales sit almost four feet off the water. The water is at least two or three feet deep, it's a long way down before your feet touch the bottom. I was beginning to think I was better off by myself. What I needed was my aluminum canoe or, better yet, a real flats boat.

I came to the conclusion that Harold and Sarah pretty much concentrated on tarpon and probably never ventured very far from Boca Grande Pass. Fair enough; at least I knew where I would be next year during tarpon season. Sarah's sister and her two nephews were headed home in the morning, so I suggested to Harold that we should wade the grass flats I had been fishing recently. That's how it went for the next couple of days.

We fished a few flats here and there and caught some nice redfish and trout. Harold managed to hook and land a ten- or eleven-pound snook, and Sarah lost a monster redfish Sunday morning on the backside just east of Blind Pass. It seemed like everyone was having fun, especially Sarah. Maybe they would spend more time in the water rather than on it and leave the gas-guzzling Mako at home.

I would miss Charlotte Harbor, but truth be told, I was going to drag Ray Moss down here next weekend. And we were going to bring my canoe this time. I wanted to fish the north end of the harbor. Unfortunately, I didn't get to spend any time there, but it looked interesting and was closer than driving down to Sanibel. The mouth of the Myakka River seemed especially intriguing. Ray kept telling me about a lake that one of his customers had overheard two guides describing at Miller's Marina on Boca Grande. It was so secret that he had to take Ray to the back room and whisper in his ear. I kept thinking to myself, damn, did he make a mistake—of all the people on the planet to tell a secret, he picked Ray Moss! I still hadn't forgotten the Humpback Bridge fiasco. The lake wasn't on the map, but according to Ray, it was on the backside of a relatively new neighborhood where most of the lots were still empty. Then he mentioned something about a hidden spillway. That got my attention.

By the time school started Monday morning, I was exhausted. I hadn't gotten much sleep over the past four days, and even though I had had a blast, I was still worried about Ralph and Brandon. Harold and Sarah were terrific people, and I didn't doubt that they would get along well with Ralph, Brandon, and Linda—that is, as long as they didn't have to fish together. Then again, I had to stop worrying about this before it drove me crazy. I had every intention of fishing with Ralph and Brandon, so Harold and Sarah would be on their own for the most part. Then again, I might spend most of my time fishing with Linda, or Linda and Sarah could always fish together. That would leave Harold to do what he wanted to do by himself. I needed to believe that things would work out.

I have no idea what happened to the days and weeks between Thanksgiving and Christmas. I remember passing driver's education and getting my restricted license. I still didn't have any real transportation; even though most of my friends had cars, I didn't think they would let me drive. However, it was a different story when it came to backing down the boat. It seems like they were more interested in making sure I could handle the boat at the boat ramp than driving the truck. I didn't mind at the time, but at some level I understood that I was being used.

The holidays were right around the corner. Christmas at our house was about as anticlimactic as two last-place teams trashing each other's roster on *Monday Night Football*. I always felt something was missing. I couldn't explain it at the time, and I still can't put my finger on it today. I hate to use the word dysfunctional, although it pretty much sums it up. My mother and my stepfather were always trying to find their niche. More than anything, I think my mother wanted to have an everyday life and a typical family. But it didn't matter how hard she tried; we would never be the Cleavers. And at one time or another, she tried almost everything. I remember when my parents spent a small fortune at a new-age camping and clothing store in downtown Sarasota. They bought a ten-man tent that must have weighed 150 pounds, two Coleman stoves, two hammocks, sleeping bags and cots for the four of us, three or four large Coleman coolers, and several lanterns. They bought so much gear that they had to have Dick Clevenger come over and build an aluminum shed behind the house to store everything.

When it came to the outdoors, my parents were clueless. If it hadn't been so sad, it might have been comical. My parents didn't have any idea where or when to camp; most important, they didn't know how to camp. It's not rocket science, but it does take a little experience. I had no idea why they were going to all the trouble and the expense. I don't remember my parents ever showing any interest in the outdoors. All they did was work. Maybe it was an attempt to bring the family together. All I know is that my mother never did anything without a reason. Somehow or other, she always expected something in return.

Finally, they decided on Oscar Sherer State Park, just south of Osprey. It was only a thirty-minute drive, so my stepfather could drive back and forth to work every day. For some unknown reason, they decided to make reservations for two weeks. The day finally came, they packed up the gear, and off they went. Two days later, they came home. I will spare you all the details, but they hated camping for a multitude of reasons. My stepfather was so pissed off that he gave me everything, including the key to the lock for the new utility shed. I never found out exactly what went wrong. They didn't seem to be talking when they walked through the front door, so it could have been a domestic dispute. Then again, it could have been the alligators. I guess it was the combination of all the work involved in setting up a camp of that size and the daily chores that probably did them in, and I am more than sure the mosquitoes played a significant role in their decision to come home early.

Several months later, my stepfather was in a local camera shop and let the owner talk him into buying a new Nikon, several expensive lenses, and a camera bag. I truly believe he thought that he would use the Nikon on something that would justify the price tag, but he never quite got the knack of taking pictures. Several months later, I was the proud owner of a new Nikon camera, lens, and bag. That was the first birthday present I liked, except maybe the cold, hard cash they usually gave me for my birthday.

In two days, Harold and Sarah would pick me up again, but this time I would be more prepared. There would be plenty of room, so I readied a small arsenal. I intended to have fifteen to eighteen rods sitting on the front porch, multiple tackle bags and boxes, several cast nets, a bait net and a mullet net, and a few travel bags of sorts. After all, we would be there for eight days this time. I knew Ralph and Brandon would bring everything but the kitchen sink. Then again, I wouldn't put it past them to bring the sink.

Harold and Sarah pulled up to our house around eleven a.m. Friday. When they got out of the Suburban, Sarah started laughing at all the tackle. But by this time, they expected as much. I didn't know it at the time, but they had been in constant contact with Ralph and Linda for the past few weeks. Harold and Sarah had been teasing me about things they had no way of knowing unless Ralph and Linda had told them.

Finally, we were headed south again. I have no idea why, but traveling south always seemed right for some reason. Ralph called me early that morning to tell me that they were already there. I could hear Linda in the background yelling at Brandon, and for some reason, I started laughing; at the same time, I was a little choked up. Even though I had made new friends and the fishing was great in Sarasota, I missed Fort Lauderdale, but I really missed the kids at the pier most of all.

In some ways, I never got over the move to Sarasota. It put a wedge between my mother and me that could never be repaired. I remember sitting on the front porch, thinking about it, I was so angry, but I wasn't going to let it ruin the next eight days. I would be old enough to go and come as I pleased in a few years.

The drive down was easy this time—we didn't spend what seemed like hours in Publix. Best of all, I didn't have to listen to Sarah's two nephews. Before I knew it, we were crossing the Sanibel Causeway. If I hadn't looked at the map on my bedroom wall that morning, I have to admit that I couldn't have told you exactly where Captiva was. I knew it was north northwest of Sanibel. You wouldn't know Captiva existed if you tied your boat up on the Fort Myers side of Sanibel Causeway and traveled north. I also thought it was odd that Harold didn't tie his boat up at the same marina this time.

My relationship with Harold and Sarah was the polar opposite of my relationship with Ralph and Linda. Harold and Sarah were incredibly kind to me and would never under any circumstances utter a disparaging remark when I was around. On the other hand, if I said something a little off-color or screwed up with Ralph, he probably would have stuck his boot up my butt.

We were slowly driving down Periwinkle Way, then we made a right turn on Tarpon Bay Road and then a left on Sanibel Captiva Road. I could only assume Harold knew where he was going. We crossed a great-looking little bridge that traversed Blind Pass. It looked so good that I wanted to stop the Suburban and check it out. We were finally on Captiva Island.

First, I noticed all the multimillion-dollar homes. They were almost impossible to miss. Next came all the schools of bait along the beach. The pelicans were having a field day. They were dropping out of the sky like dive-bombers. The terns were skimming in and out of all the pelicans, scooping up the smaller bait. They were doing their best to pick up what was left from the carnage. The gulls were yapping so loudly you could hear them from the road.

Late afternoon thunderstorms were starting to build far out in the Gulf of Mexico. The towering thunderheads simultaneously looked threatening and a little foreboding, yet incredibly beautiful. The water was as calm as glass. I knew there had to be fish in there. After we made a few twists and turns, Harold made a sharp right, and we followed a long, winding driveway that seemed to go on forever. It finally opened up on the bay.

The house was amazing, or maybe I should say houses. I didn't know homes like this existed. Then I saw Ralph's truck, and Brandon on the dock carrying dozens of rods and reels. Ralph and Linda walked out of the front door, waved, and came up to the truck to shake hands with Harold and Sarah. Linda ran over to my side of the truck and gave me a long hug. I didn't want to let go. Before I could say anything, Ralph came up from behind me, put me in a bear hug, lifted me off the ground, and started laughing. Brandon yelled something from the docks and then came running as fast as he could in flip-flops.

The first question out of Brandon's mouth was about tiki bars and girls, and then the conversation moved on to surfing. I hated to tell him that I had no idea if Captiva had tiki bars, but it sure didn't have any surf. However, it did have outstanding fishing, and the grass flats were tailor-made for fly-fishing. I spent the next hour unloading my gear and telling them about my last trip to Sanibel. Brandon was dragging my fishing gear to the back porch, and Linda was unpacking my bags, folding my clothes, and stuffing them in the dresser. Then Ralph and I went over about half a dozen charts of Charlotte Harbor that he had spread out on the kitchen table. Harold and Sarah were unloading the Mako and settling into their new accommodations.

My room was almost as big as my family house on Siesta Key. The house was enormous! It reminded me of a hotel, anything but someone's private residence. When I finally made my way to the back deck, I was speechless. The house consisted of three distinct levels. Everything opened to the bay. The upper deck was an observation platform; the second deck held the swimming pool, and the lower deck led out to the boat docks. There were three flats boats; two, which belonged to the owner, were up on davits. Ralph's skiff was tied to the first dock. Then I noticed the lights on the end of the dock.

This week was going to be fun! Harold pulled the Mako into an empty parking spot next to the caretaker's house and left it there. At that point, I didn't think he would put the boat in the water. Instead, I think it was there if someone wanted to go offshore to bottom fish. I have to admit that sounded interesting. I hadn't tugged on a big grouper in what seemed like years.

About that time, the chef and housekeeping crew showed up. Fifteen minutes later, the groundskeeper pulled up with a giant Christmas tree in the bed of the pickup. It never dawned on me that today was Christmas Eve. It only took the caretaker and the housekeeper an hour or so to decorate the tree. Linda and Sarah took part once in a while and offered a few suggestions to make it feel like it was our tree. It felt weird in some ways—we had a tree, but we didn't have any presents under it, so we decided we would celebrate Christmas on New Year's Eve. That would give everyone a week to come up with a few goofy gifts—nothing expensive, just a few odds and ends. It would be nice to ring in the New Year with new friends and old.

The night seemed perfect. Everyone was getting along well, as if they were old friends who hadn't seen each other in years. We had dinner outside on the upper deck. The outside lights were on, including the dock lights. You could see the shrimp starting to float by. I knew what Brandon was thinking. The snook were beginning to stack up down current of the shrimp, so it was only a matter of time before he sneaked out the back door, and tiptoed down to the dock (as if no one would notice) to pilfer a few snook.

Dinner was incredible! It started with conch chowder, a small Caesar salad with homemade dressing, and a wicker basket full of freshly made French baguettes. A few minutes later, the chef came from the kitchen wearing a broad smile and bearing the main course, a huge fresh red snapper stuffed with crabmeat and shrimp accompanied by dirty rice and butter beans. Dessert was a large slice of homemade key lime pie smothered in whipped cream and a small scoop of key lime sorbet. Of course, I was drinking coffee, and everyone else was drinking pinot grigio except Ralph. He was drinking scotch and soda. If you are wondering how I could remember what everyone was drinking, it's because I tasted everyone's wine—just a sip to see which one I liked best, in case someone felt sorry for me and offered me a drink.

Dinner lasted for hours, and finally, somebody suggested that we move down to the docks and let the chef and housekeeper clean up and go home. The girls tried to help clear the table, but the housekeepers seemed offended. Eventually, we learned that they were there for the duration, staying in one of the guesthouses with the groundskeeper. The service was a little over the top, but Ralph didn't think much about it. He had been guiding the owner and his family for years and had grown accustomed to such lavish treatment.

Slowly but surely, everyone drifted back to their rooms, except Brandon and me. We lasted a few more hours, then called it a night. I thought it was a little weird that no one mentioned getting up at the crack of dawn to go fishing the next morning. According to Brandon, everyone would sleep in and have a late breakfast, then load the boats and head out after lunch. I was lying in bed trying to sleep, but it wasn't happening. I didn't know if it was the alcohol or all the snook stacked under the lights just waiting to be harassed. I was also thinking about dinner; I can't tell you how often I heard my name mentioned. It was as if everyone was getting to know each other via all the conversations they had had over the past several months. At least no one seemed to be pissed at me. Finally, I decided to crawl out of bed and say "hello" to the snook.

Giant gumbo-limbo trees were everywhere—some people call them copperwoods, and I have even heard them called turpentine trees, especially by people from Central America. Orchids were hanging from all three decks. The owner's wife was a renowned botanist who had made a name for herself but eventually walked away to enjoy the good life. The place was smothered in flowers she had collected on her travels throughout the tropics while her husband was off chasing permit. If you looked off the back decks, you could see giant red mangroves and oyster bars. The property was thick and almost dripping with organic scents and saturated colors.

You could practically taste them on your palate. It was a complex assault on all your senses at the same time. I just stood there, absorbing everything like a sponge. It was intoxicating. There was no sign of the real world. For all practical purposes, the property could have been sitting on an unknown estuary deep in the jungles of Belize. Yet, it was beautiful in every sense of the word. Sanibel and Captiva had been under a constant assault from the Northeast and the Midwest for the past sixty or seventy years. Yet, you could still find little gems like this tucked away in the nooks and crannies on some of Florida's most remote barrier islands.

Stuck in the Muck at Low Tide

$\mathcal{F}$orty-some years later, the invasive species have almost destroyed Sanibel and Captiva Island. The population continues to grow at an unbelievable rate. In season, the traffic is so bad that nothing moves; it's a perpetual traffic jam. Yet people continue to pay incredible prices and exorbitant taxes to live there. Every time someone builds a new home, another piece of landscape disappears. The traffic gets worse, the pollution grows, and yet the people on Sanibel and Captiva blame everyone but themselves. How bad does it have to get before everyone wakes up? That's an easy question to answer—we are long past the point of no return. Sanibel and Captiva will never recover. It will never be the same place I spent years fishing and exploring as a young man. How and why we let it happen has always been a mystery to me, but it wasn't just Sanibel and Captiva. It was the whole of South Florida.

When I look back at the eight days we spent together on Captiva, I almost get sick to my stomach. Day after day, we explored Charlotte Harbor and never scratched the surface. Every day was a new experience. We were overwhelmed by the beauty and fertility of the harbor, especially the passes. I remember Brandon and I were staked out at the mouth of Gasparilla Pass on an incoming tide one morning, pitching flies to snook after snook as they rounded the mouth of the pass, following the incoming tide. We must have spent two or three hours there and never hooked one. I had no idea where they were going. I always wondered what might have happened if I had pitched a live shrimp in front of them.

Later that afternoon, when the tide started dropping, we were staked out on a shallow grass flat just east of the mouth of the Myakka River casting Johnson Silver Minnows at monster redfish. Together we caught seven or eight huge redfish that afternoon. We got lucky that day and poled off the flat right before the tide completely dropped out. The last thing you wanted to do was get stuck in the muck at low tide, especially in the evening. The mosquitoes would have had a feast. I kept thinking maybe we should have kept a few redfish for dinner, but then again, I didn't want to insult the chef. I fished with Brandon most of the time, but I saved the last two days to fish with Ralph and Linda. The following two days couldn't have been more different from each other.

The day I spent with Ralph on the water was all about fishing and nothing but fishing. In some ways, Ralph was as intense as any fisherman I have been around. He was always trying to put me on bigger, better fish. He was a poling maniac, and a man of few words. But, of course, if you were paying Ralph $600 a day to put you on fish, that's exactly who you would want on the poling platform. We fished a little over thirteen hours that day, ran from one end of the harbor to the other, came back along the gulf, and made our way through Stump Pass just in time for dinner. We caught so many redfish and trout I lost count somewhere around lunchtime.

That night we celebrated Christmas and rang in the New Year together. We were up late, and I don't want to mention any names, but not everyone fished the next day. Linda and I left the dock around seven the following morning. It was our last day together, and I wanted to spend as much time on the water with her as possible. I was going to spend the day on the poling platform; it was my turn to do something for her. She had always been my sounding board when I needed someone to chat with, and I would bet she knew me better than my parents.

I wanted to run down to Gasparilla Pass and, if the gulf was calm, work our way back up to Boca Grande Pass and fish the beach along the way for snook. The gulf was so flat that it looked like a mirror. We turned south and started working our way along the beach. We could see giant schools of bait being ripped to shreds just off the shore. I jumped on it and tried to get there before the bait disappeared.

When we got close enough to make a decent cast, I put the engine in neutral and shut it down. Linda had already started stripping line off the reel and false casting. Linda could cast a fly rod as well as any fly fishermen I had ever met. She was so smooth, you could tell she was having a blast. Linda put the Clouser right in the middle of the bait and then let it sink to the bottom. She started stripping the fly, and almost immediately got slammed. She set the hook, and the fish took off like a rocket sled on wheels. The line came tight. She cleared the line without any trouble, and the reel started screaming. About that time, I saw a bunch of big jacks slicing their way through the bait. At first, I thought she might have a big jack on, but this was different. The fish on Linda's line was headed for the open gulf. It didn't look like it would stop any time soon.

I started the engine and gave her a chance to get some line back on the reel. By the time I got the engine started, the fish was already several hundred yards into the backing. We followed the fish for the next forty-five minutes. We were almost a quarter mile offshore when the fish finally turned and headed back to the beach. I just wanted to get on top of the fish, so I could see what it was. The fish finally turned parallel to the beach heading south toward Boca Grande. We were almost on top of it when Linda started yelling, "It's a permit, it's a permit."

I kept thinking, *there is no way it could be a permit*, but what did I know? If Linda said it was a permit, it was.

The closer we got, the larger the fish looked. Then I got a good look at it. Sure enough, it was a permit, but not just any permit. It was huge. I knew you could catch a permit on the wrecks offshore, but I never knew they came anywhere near the beaches. The lactic acid had to be building in the permit's muscles by this point. It looked exhausted! We were about ten feet from the beach. The water was starting to get shallow, so I told Linda to step out of the skiff, and then I would drop the anchor and tail the fish.

I had never tailed a permit of any size, much less one this big, even though I had watched Ted Williams land and tail a big permit on *The American Sportsman* with Curt Gowdy a few years before. We were both on the beach by this time, and the permit was only several feet away. I tried to guide it a little closer to shore, and then I grabbed the tail and hung on for dear life. It wasn't as bad as I thought it would be; the poor fish was bone tired. When I grabbed the leader, the fly fell out. I was on my knees, trying to revive the permit when Linda grabbed her pack and took out the camera and started taking pictures. The permit was beginning to show signs of life, and a few minutes later, it swam away.

I could only guess, but I thought the fish was somewhere in the twenty- to twenty-five-pound range. It was the largest permit I had seen outside of the Miami Seaquarium. Linda hugged me. I thought that being married to a guide, especially Ralph, he would have put her on a lot of big permit by now, but this was her first permit. Years later, I developed a passion for permit on the fly. It's like a thirst that can't be quenched. It became a never-ending pursuit of one of the world's greatest game fish.

Later that night, we were all sitting around the dinner table, swapping fishing stories. The last eight days seemed like a blur. No one wanted it to end, especially me. Linda and Ralph were on the quiet side for most of the night. They hardly said anything, and after dinner, Ralph and Linda walked out on the upper deck to talk. Ten minutes went by, then fifteen. A few minutes later, Linda came up behind me, grabbed my hand, and walked me outside to the deck where Ralph was waiting. She asked if I wanted to move back to Fort Lauderdale and live with them. Brandon was away at college, so the house had plenty of room. I could finish school and then decide what I wanted to do, or where I wanted to live, and if I wanted to go to college, they would help in any way they could.

It almost floored me. I didn't know what to say. How do you respond to an offer like that? If Ralph and Linda had made the same offer six months before, I would have packed my bags and moved back to Fort Lauderdale in a heartbeat, though I knew my mother would have fought me every inch of the way. Unfortunately, by this time I had other plans, and they didn't have anything to do with Fort Lauderdale. I spent the next half hour trying to explain what I had in mind. Ralph thought I was crazy, but Linda just smiled, kissed me on the cheek, and said good luck. I knew that of all the people on the planet, she would understand.

The next morning came quickly, too quickly for some. The libations had flowed with impunity that last night, and I think a few of us might have pushed our limit a little too far. I set the alarm clock so I could get up at four-thirty to catch the tide change and rip a few lips under the lights on the dock. It was nice to have the lights on the dock to myself for once. I fished until the sun started peeking over the mangroves. The sunrise was stunning. The snook kept biting for another half hour or so after the sun was up. It was the perfect way to end the trip.

At least some of us had tried to pack the night before. Breakfast was almost ready, and the groundskeeper was spraying down the flats skiffs. The housekeeper was carrying bag after bag down the stairs and stacking them on the front porch. That way, we could pull Ralph's truck and Harold's Suburban up to the front door and load everyone's gear. I volunteered to run Ralph's skiff back up to the public launch and drive it up on the trailer. Linda jumped at the opportunity to go with me. After a huge breakfast, I helped Harold line up the Suburban with the Mako, hook up the trailer, and tie it down. Brandon finally crawled out of bed. He wasn't looking too well and the last thing on his mind was breakfast, even though that's exactly what he needed. I would miss Brandon more than he could ever understand, but I think Linda and Ralph understood very well.

After breakfast, everyone said their good-byes. There was talk of doing this again next year, but I knew it would never happen. It was a miracle that it happened this year. Linda and I jumped in Ralph's skiff. This time Linda was driving. She idled out of the little estuary and jumped on it. The engine was running wide open, and we were barely skimming over the grass and oyster bars. Linda kept adjusting the trim tabs to keep us from scraping the bottom of the skiff. She knew what she was doing. About halfway to the boat ramp, Linda put the engine in neutral and came to a complete stop.

She asked again if I would reconsider Ralph's and her offer to move back to Fort Lauderdale. I was so tempted, but it just didn't fit my plans. I remember driving over the Sanibel Causeway heading home that day; I couldn't stop thinking about Ralph and Linda, much less Brandon.

It was time to go home; school started tomorrow, and I still had a lot of unpacking before I could finally get some sleep. The adrenalin was still pumping, and it would be tough to go to school and pretend the last eight days never happened. For some reason, I kept humming John Lennon's song *Lucy in the Sky with Diamonds.*

It just seemed appropriate.

• 31 •

Frank the Net

here comes a time when life is a little overwhelming. The days seem to blur into weeks, the weeks seem to melt into months, and before you know it, you're a year older, and the beat goes on. I have also heard that the older you get, the faster time seems to fly. I'm assuming that it has to do with physiological time and not the actual time on the clock. I needed to slow down, take a deep breath, drop out of warp, and come to terms with the fact that you can't do all things for all the people all the time.

The ultimate goal in life should be happiness. You need to wrap yourself around anything and everything you possibly can that makes you happy. If not, you will wake up one day and find out that you flushed your life down the toilet, and by that time, your life essentially is over. Unfortunately, it seems to be the norm, not the exception. In the end, I think it's nothing more than the search for meaning in your life.

Over the years, I have slowly come to the conclusion that fishing is just a conduit to nature. It's the vehicle that allows me to travel the world and experience nature in ways and places I could only have dreamed of when I was a teenager growing up in Fort Lauderdale and Sarasota. That's not to say that I don't love fishing. I do, probably much more than anyone could ever imagine.

For me, it's become more of a philosophical approach to the way I perceive nature, and it could be considered a spiritual quest of sorts. It's almost a mystical journey. Regardless of what people want to believe, we are part of nature, no better or no worse. When people start thinking they're not a part of nature or believe that they are more important than nature, that causes all the problems. It's nothing more than a rationalization. It allows people to stand by and watch the demise of the majority of the wildlife on the planet. We pollute the lakes and rivers. We trash the oceans and harvest the fish until we drive the majority of species into extinction. I will never understand why and how we stood by and let this happen. Maybe it's too complex to wrap your mind around. Or perhaps we don't care. People will often tell you the problem is too big for one person. Then I think to myself, did Ed Abbey make a difference? Did Gary Snyder make a difference? Did Jacques Cousteau make a difference?

What about Rachel Carson, Henry David Thoreau, and Edward O. Wilson? Did any of them make a difference? Tough question. I'm not sure there is a good answer. I think they influenced many people, but in the end, did it help? I think we are exponentially better off after reading their prose and poetry, but does it inspire people to save the natural world?

Unfortunately, we seem to be significantly outnumbered by those who profit heavily off what natural resources we have left. Further, we are surrounded by false prophets, people who pretend they want to save the planet but instead want the ultimate power over it, which also means us. They want to decide what's good and bad for the environment.

On the other hand, John Muir single-handedly convinced Abraham Lincoln to save and set aside the California redwoods and eventually created Yosemite National Park. Archie Carr convinced the Mexican government and other Central American countries to abolish their commercial fishing practices to save sea turtles.

Jane Goodall is another one. Beginning at the age of twenty-six, she prevented the slaughter of hundreds, if not thousands of chimpanzees in Tanzania. Marjory Stoneman Douglas almost single-handedly saved parcel after parcel of land throughout the Everglades until her death in 1998, though she hardly ever spent time there. She didn't have to live in the Glades to understand the importance of saving this watershed, and what it meant to the Everglades and Florida Bay. I'm sure that thousands of unsung heroes around the world took it upon themselves to stop environmental atrocities. If we can't be inspired by these people to do something, what hope is there?

I stopped by Economy Tackle on the way home from school and spent quality time with Ray. It would take hours trying to explain the last ten days. We talked about the fishing in Gasparilla Pass, Little Gasparilla Pass, and the mouth of the Myakka River. He couldn't stop asking about Charlotte Harbor. He wanted to know about Boca Grande, and the phosphate docks. Then we started talking about the fly-fishing possibilities, and there just wasn't enough time left in the day to fill him in on all the potential fishing spots. So, we decided to catch the incoming tide Saturday morning and fish Little Gasparilla Pass at sunup, then have lunch at Miller's Marina. After lunch, we would head over to a hidden lake his buddy kept telling him about. If I was lucky, we might find the spillway that his friend had whispered about several months ago.

This depended on Ray's beat-up old Florida Power and Light truck. At least we were headed south. This would be the first time I had driven along the harbor, much less through Englewood. When I visited Sanibel with Harold and Sarah, we took U.S. 41 south to Fort Myers and then the Sanibel Causeway over to Sanibel and Captiva Island. This time, Ray and I took U.S. 41 south of Venice and then took the cutoff at a place called Whiskey Corners. The locals named it Whiskey Corners because a nightclub is in the middle of the fork in the road. We followed 776, the Old Englewood Road, south toward Placida, and then turned right at the Boca Grande Causeway onto Boca Grande Island.

Three distinct bridges on Boca Grande cross different parts of Charlotte Harbor. The middle bridge crossed Gasparilla Pass. The third bridge crossed a channel that eventually opened up to an incredible maze of mangrove islands and small creeks. The small creeks were almost impenetrable because of all the oyster bars and mud flats. It was a beautiful place to explore with a canoe, especially on a strong incoming tide. It gave you a glimpse of what old Florida must have been like—and could be again—if the residents of South Florida could slow the impending wave of humanity that was headed their way. It was almost claustrophobic, especially on hot, humid days without sea breezes. The mosquitoes were so bad you needed a transfusion after you paddled out. Either that or you slathered on enough bug dope that you almost died from the copious DEET.

An old railroad trestle snaked its way through the labyrinth of mangrove islands and oyster bars. The middle section that once crossed the bay had long since been removed. I assume that was about the same time the phosphate industry pulled out of Boca Grande. It's hard to believe that the Boca Grande I experienced in the early seventies was relatively undeveloped; it was primarily open beaches, campgrounds, and one or two marinas. The only time I can remember real crowds was during the tarpon tournaments that took place every spring and summer. Then Boca Grande Pass turned into a living nightmare. At the right tide, you could virtually walk across all the charter boats to Cayo Costa, the island due south of Boca Grande. It's amazing what money can do to fishing and worse, its effect on fishermen.

We had two choices. We could fish from the top of the bridges and jig for pompano until the tide changed, or walk the beaches and fish for snook. I had fished the front side of Boca Grande the previous week with Linda, which was where she caught her first permit on the fly. Brandon and I had spent several mornings pitching flies at snook along the beach with little to show for our time and effort. Jigging for pompano sounded interesting. I hadn't caught a pompano in years, and according to Ray, he had never caught anything that resembled a pompano. So, we decided to spend time on the middle bridge; if that didn't work out, we would fish the third bridge. We could always walk the beach or have breakfast at Miller's Marina.

Ray pulled his old truck off the road and parked it in what looked like a gravel lot beside the bridge. We didn't see any "No Parking" signs. That was always a good sign. People were a lot more reasonable about parking in those days before the carpetbaggers, robber barons, and land developers decided it was bad for business if the bridge going over to Boca Grande was lined with fishermen. The locals would usually slow down and ask you if you were catching anything. Sometimes they would even pull off the road and walk back up the bridge to look at your catch or shoot the bull.

The railings were extremely low for a bridge. You could sit on the railings or straddle them while you rigged your rod. There weren't sidewalks as such, only an eighteen-inch slab of concrete to navigate. Sometimes the distance between the fishermen and the cars was almost indistinguishable. It could get up close and personal quickly. Ray and I were sitting on the railing tying on a couple of pompano jigs when we heard a loud rumbling coming down the road. It sounded like someone was having difficulty shifting gears—grinding metal on metal—and unfortunately, the abrasive sound of a vehicle in need of a new clutch.

An old International Harvester flatbed that had seen better days came barreling up the bridge, huffing and puffing, coughing up black and gray exhaust. It barely made it over the bridge. The truck carried five or six coolers strapped down on the flatbed, half a dozen laundry baskets, and about twenty pairs of white tennis shoes in various stages of decay. I didn't get much of a chance to see the driver, but he didn't look very enthusiastic about seeing us on the bridge. As he crossed the bridge to the other side, he slammed on his brakes, pulled off the road, and slid into the dirt parking lot. There he sat for the next half hour. Eventually, he got out, walked up to the far side of the bridge, and sat there on the railing, arms crossed, glaring at us as if we had done something to offend him.

Ray kept fishing as if he weren't there. It was hard to believe that someone could be that laid back with this guy watching us. I decided to ignore him, too.

Right then, I had to teach Ray how to work a pompano jig. I didn't think he would catch too many pompano ripping the jig across the surface of the water. But of course, catching a mackerel wasn't exactly out of the realm of possibility this time of year either. I hooked a nice pompano on my second cast while teaching Ray how to bounce the jig along the bottom. I was using a Mitchell 410 spinning reel made in France and a seven-foot Lew's Speed Stick spooled with twelve-pound test Trilene XLT. It was the perfect combination for jigging for pompano. Even a two-pound fish could peel off thirty or forty feet of line on the first run. I had forgotten just how strong pompano were.

Three or four minutes later, I had the fish straight up and down. It was almost too big to flip. I thought about walking it down to the seawall and landing it with the net, but in the end, I managed to flip it onto the bridge. I took the jig out, ran the pompano down to the truck, and put it on ice. On the way back, I was watching Ray, and he still didn't have the hang of it. I don't remember it being that hard; I thought it was rather intuitive the first time I tried bouncing a jig along the bottom.

He was bouncing the jig all right, but every time he reeled in the slack line, it kept working its way up the water column. I tried to make him understand that he needed to let the jig fall back to the bottom. It's easy, especially if you let the tide do the work for you. All you had to do was open the bail and let the jig fall, and when the line came slack, take a few turns on the reel or manually flip the bail and start jigging. Every time I tried to demonstrate the proper technique, I managed to hook and land another pompano. I caught three fish on five casts. Little Gasparilla pass was loaded with 'em.

Our new companion, the International Harvester driver, kept getting closer. Then I heard Ray screaming for help! He was standing tight against the railing, holding his rod with one hand, and his other hand was on the spool, trying to palm it. Ray was doing his best to slow down the fish, but there was absolutely nothing anyone could do to help him. He was about to get spooled.

The only line still attached to the spool was the last loop and the knot. I was doing everything I could to get a look at the fish. I thought it might have been a giant stingray or a leopard ray. I can't tell you how often I accidentally snagged a big stingray in the butt and thought I had a monster snook instead. Ray's rod shattered into a million tiny fiberglass pieces, and then the line broke. It's the ultimate humiliation when someone tells you that you just got spooled. I always thought it was better to have hooked and lost a fish than never having hooked the fish at all.

Ray was an emotional mess. He was one part excited and one part angry, but what he wanted to know was if I had another spinning outfit he could borrow. About that time, I looked up, and it seemed our friend had come down to help or, at the very least, put in his two cents.

He introduced himself as Frank the Net. My first impression was, who names a kid Frank the Net? It never dawned on me that "Net" meant cast net. He was a little intimidating at first. He was a big guy, and he had a habit of getting in your face. On the other hand, he seemed harmless in a goofy sort of way. He didn't seem interested in Ray or his herculean effort to stop whatever he hooked, regardless of whether he had snagged a big stingray. It destroyed Ray's outfit, and you don't get to experience that very often. It's happened to me a few times on Anglin's Pier, and it took me days to get over the emotional drain. The difference was that I saw the fish that did the damage. That's like pouring salt on a fresh wound.

Frank was probably thinking the same thing I was thinking. It almost had to be a big stingray. But he was more interested in my three pompano and what I intended to do with them. From the looks of his attire and his transportation, he could be living in the Harvester. I was more than willing to give Frank my three pompano. What little I knew about Frank, it might have been his breakfast. Then again, Ray's truck was in worse condition, but his house and property were worth as much as three or four hundred thousand dollars.

We had a short conversation, and before I could tell Frank he could have a few fish, especially if I caught a couple more, Frank bolted back down the bridge waving his arm, beckoning me to follow him to his truck. He opened the door, grabbed a copy of the first *Florida Sportsman* ever published, and gave it to me. Frank's mug was on the cover throwing a cast net. Unfortunately, I didn't understand the importance of being on the cover of the first issue of any fishing magazine, but the last thing I wanted to do was insult him. Frank thought it was important, and that's all that counted.

For the life of me, I can't tell you his real name. Everybody knew him as Frank the Net. I just called him Frank. I didn't understand why he seemed interested in me and not Ray, other than the three pompano in the cooler. We walked back up on the bridge, and I started rummaging through my tackle bag. I grabbed a handful of pompano jigs and some bucktails that I tied and gave them to Frank. He threw everything into his pocket and walked silently off the bridge. A few minutes later, he came walking back carrying two five-gallon buckets. He dropped them at my feet and told me to enjoy them. I opened the buckets, and I was dumbfounded—I didn't know what to say. In each bucket was a cast net, an eight-foot bait net, and a twelve-foot mullet net.

We still had several good hours of the incoming tide to fish. If we were lucky, we might catch a few more pompano. Frank went back to his truck, grabbed his spinning rod, and the three of us fished together until the tide started dropping out. Gasparilla Pass turned out to be an incredible fishery.

We caught half a dozen more pompano, but we also caught several nice jacks, dozens of ladyfish, and the occasional bluefish. Frank kept telling us about the spring cobia run and all the big redfish that run through the pass in the fall. I asked him about the snook fishing, and he just shrugged his shoulders in disgust. He didn't seem to care for snook.

• 32 •

Another Day in Paradise

$\mathscr{R}$ay and I talked Frank into having lunch with us at the Laugh A Lot restaurant. It was either there, the Pink Elephant, or a burger at Miller's Marina. (Two years later, a drunken patron backed over the gas pumps at Miller's and then drove right into the tackle store. The fuel pumps exploded, and the fire burned the marina to the ground. Miller's never reopened.)

Brandon and I had filled the skiff with gas at Miller's a few times the previous week. The marina was the local hangout for all the captains and mates who fished Boca Grande Pass. Miller's Marina was a treasure trove of tarpon lore.

Some of these guys were third- and fourth-generation crackers. I should have had the foresight and understanding to see what was happening around me. The Boca Grande I knew would fade into history in a few years. The families would leave or disappear from the landscape, and their history would be permanently altered or lost altogether. Over the years, dozens of books would be written about the fishing culture that once permeated Boca Grande. Unfortunately, the oral history of Boca Grande is, at best, a fleeting moment.

We pulled into the parking lot at the Laugh A Lot at about eleven o'clock. The tide had just changed direction. We walked across the street and watched an unbelievable amount of water pouring out of Boca Grande Pass. The pass was empty at the time, but it would look like Madison Square Garden at rush hour on steroids in a few months. We walked in, and half a dozen fishermen and beach bums waved and said hi to Frank. Over the next two hours, we probably met twenty-five or thirty people who seemed to know him intimately. I didn't know whether Frank was a local icon or an infamous character like Ed Watson. Everyone loved Ed Watson right up to when the town members of Chokoloskee met him at the docks at Smallwood Store and filled him full of buckshot.

We shared a giant meatball pizza big enough for five or six hungry people. Frank kept describing all the ins and outs of Boca Grande—places we needed to fish and places that looked fishy but rarely produced. Then he talked at length about El Jobean and the Myakka River. For some reason, Frank loved the river mouths. I had come to that same conclusion years before. If the major estuaries were left alone, undeveloped, they would continue to work as nurseries to provide the game fish for Charlotte Harbor. That was a big if.

We asked him about the spillway Ray's buddy kept describing. According to Frank, it wasn't a real spillway; it was more like a conservation dike. Freshwater only poured over the top of the dam during heavy summer rains, but if we wanted to fish a great spillway, he knew of one behind the Winn-Dixie in Port Charlotte. I still wanted to know how to hack our way into the spillway/conservation dike. Getting to the bayside of the spillway with a canoe sounded better than hacking through a maze of mangroves and mudflats. Knowing the South Florida Water District as I do, I can't believe they built any dam or dike without access for maintenance or repair.

The access was easy, and when the water was running, it was full of snook. From what Frank could tell, the conservation dike wasn't heavily fished. He also described what sounded like hundreds of miles of freshwater canals, full of bass and bluegills, that ran in and out of the neighborhoods in Port Charlotte. Ray asked about the lake that ran into the conservation dike, and according to Frank, it did exist. Essentially, Placida and South Englewood were full of empty subdivisions with man-made canals and lakes, and they all held fish. He also heard rumors that the lake in question was full of big redfish and snook.

Lunch lasted for hours. By the time everyone had finished, it was getting too late in the day to find the lake, much less fish there. Before we left, Frank asked in a sinister sort of way for my phone number, in case he needed to get in touch with me. I grudgingly gave it to him and reminded him I was still in high school and I didn't have transportation.

Ray and I tried to get down to Boca Grande at least once a week. Every time we fished the pass, Frank managed to show up. We tried our hand at camping there one weekend, but the mosquitoes were unbearable. There just wasn't enough bug dope on the planet to turn back the hordes of blood-sucking vampires. Even in the winter months, the mosquitoes were unbearable. For the most part, we followed Frank around the island from one spot to another. He was always on the move. Frank was driven by the tides, and not necessarily the incoming tides. We fished places on various stages of outgoing tides and the occasional dead tide, but only for a few minutes at a time. He obviously had been doing this for a long time. The more we fished together, the more I learned about Frank. He would never tell you the whole story, just bits and pieces.

According to Frank, he was born in Tampa and attended the University of Florida. Six long years later, he left school with a master's degree in business administration. This is where things get a little hazy. Frank told me he moved back to Tampa and went to work for a relative selling real estate. I have no idea what went wrong, or if anything went wrong. Frank dropped everything, packed up his family, and headed down to the Florida Keys. After settling in the Islamorada/Marathon area, he started making nets. Frank learned how to make cast nets, seine nets, and shrimp nets of all shapes and sizes for commercial fishermen.

Eventually, he knew everyone in the fishing industry who might be important to his livelihood, especially the commercial fishermen. Frank was the original barterer. The Frank the Net I knew would trade anything if it served his purpose or need. He was continually trading his skills for goods and services from the commercial fishermen, backcountry guides, charter boat captains, carpenters, plumbers, and more.

Frank eventually ended up with a large skiff of sorts. I'm flying by the seat of my pants now. I have no accurate description of the boat, but from what Frank told me, it had to be big enough to carry dozens of five-gallon buckets loaded with cast nets and a live well big enough to keep ten to fifteen dozen mullet alive. I'm not even sure the boat had a motor. This much I know for sure: Frank kept complaining about how difficult the boat was to pole in and out of the mangrove creeks and bays. This was in the early fifties. The Florida Keys were still largely undeveloped. He either drifted with the tides or poled his way into the shallow creeks and bays, looking for silver mullet. At that time, commercial cast nets didn't have drawstrings. Frank would throw his net over a school of mullet, connect a crab trap float to the top of the net, move to the next school of mullet, and do the same thing repeatedly until he ran out of cast nets. Later, he would go back to retrieve the mullet from the nets. Once the live well was full, he would make his way back to the truck and transfer the mullet to a larger live well. After breakfast somewhere, he would meet the charter boat captains and mates at the marina and sell the live mullet to the highest bidder.

As the years went by, Frank's kids started getting involved in the drug culture in the Keys. But, of course, it wasn't only the Florida Keys; it was the whole of South Florida. So, Frank grabbed his family and moved them to Englewood, Florida. At that time, Englewood was nothing more than a secluded little fishing village tucked away between Placida and Boca Grande.

The Frank the Net saga began. It was anything but boring. It had its ups and downs, but Frank was one of the most iconic fishermen in the Florida

Keys. He was Charlie Waterman, Flip Pallot, and Lefty Kreh wrapped up in one person. In some ways, Frank was Mark Sosin reincarnated. He could be cantankerous and, at times, belligerent to other fishermen, but if he liked you, he would do anything for you. Frank was one of the most generous fishermen I had ever met. Over the years, I have run into other fishermen who seemed to be made from the same mold. Most of them lived a ragtag life in the Florida Keys or out West in places like Montana and Wyoming. Yet, they seem to have one thing in common, regardless of what you might think of them—they lived life, good or bad, on their terms.

• 33 •

The Life of the Rich and Shameless

$\mathcal{S}$pring break was right around the corner. From what I could tell, I didn't have a lot of options as I had waited until the last possible moment to make plans. Maybe it was a subconscious decision, or perhaps I just wanted to stay close to home. It wasn't always that way. Growing up in Fort Lauderdale, I knew exactly what I would do during spring break: hang out at Anglin's Pier with all the other pier rats. If there happened to be a decent break, I would spend the morning surfing and then fish in the afternoon. If not, I would spend the entire day fishing or hang out in the tackle shop. Most nights, I would have dinner and crash at Brandon's house, sometimes with or without Brandon. According to Linda, I always had a standing invitation. Unless something drastic happened, I would spend the entire nine days either on or around the pier.

Unfortunately, Siesta Key didn't provide me with very many options.

Though lack of transportation severely limited me, spring break gave me a chance to spend more time turning over rocks, fishing all the nooks and crannies that make up Siesta Key. I wanted to attack the island piece by piece by myself. The only thing that could ruin a good day of fishing was another fisherman. If you limited the number of fishermen, anything was possible. Fishing has always been a solitary pursuit, regardless of how many fishermen tag along. More often than not, it's been between you, the fish, and Mother Nature, and in some cases, a guide. I would do everything in my power to spend the next nine days on the water alone, without interruption, to slow down, relax, and remember. Sometimes I think we forget why we fish. Often it becomes little more than a habit we take for granted.

I wanted to slide my canoe into the canal behind our house, then spend the next several days floating in and out with the tides. By the time we moved to Sarasota, Siesta Key had been sliced up, plowed over, and divided into a multitude of smaller neighborhoods. Each neighborhood contained miles and miles of canals and seawalls that seemed to go on forever. Every house on the water came equipped with a dock, its size and complexity dependent on your financial status. Every dock was different, and all were in various stages of repair. Saltwater plays hell with wooden docks, which have always required time, energy, and an enormous amount of money. Boats of all shapes and sizes were moored throughout the labyrinth of canals, from thirteen-foot Boston Whalers to seventy-foot battlewagons.

Some of the larger boats had tuna towers that seemed to reach for the sky, although I would bet that most of them were for show only. They were nothing more than a status symbol, and anyone who has ever climbed a tuna tower knows exactly what I am talking about. More often than not, the size of your boat depends on which side of the little bridges you live. The Grande Canal opened up to Roberts Bay in several locations. The people who lived on Roberts Bay were free to own any size boat they could afford. The people who lived on the west side of the bridges were restricted by the neighborhood bridges' height and the tide.

The size of the docks and their various stages of repair had little to do with the size and number of fish a dock attracted. In my experience, the docks closer to the bay held larger fish, seemed to be more affected by tides, and consistently fished better. If you took your time and slowed down, boat docks always paid dividends. Docks on the west side of Roberts Bay held mostly small snook, redfish, and in the winter, speckled sea trout. Occasionally in the morning, you would run into schools of marauding jacks wreaking havoc with the finger mullet along the seawalls. Besides the occasional tourist, I was usually the only one on the water in the early morning.

The docks on the bayside sound fantastic, and for the most part, they were, but provided a crapshoot at best. It was a long paddle from my house, and chances were good that a guide would be staked out, or even worse, tied off to the dock I wanted to fish. I didn't have a chance in a canoe, and from what I have experienced over the years, the guides could care less about the general public. All they were really interested in was the fat cat in the boat paying them $600 a day to fill the cooler. Of course, if I were the guide, the only person I would care about is that fat cat, too. It's all a matter of perspective.

As the years ticked by, the number of guides seemed to double, sometimes triple, every year. The exponential explosion of guides and the demise of the fisheries appeared to mirror the population growth of South Florida. Everybody seems to want to be a guide, and some not only guided but also hocked real estate while running in and out of the multimillion-dollar neighborhoods. The sad part was that it was so pervasive that a fifteen-year-old kid could understand what was happening.

I could spend all morning pounding the mangrove shoreline with plastic baits and plugs or work the docks with jigs. Sometimes the seawalls and docks were strangled with mangroves that started from a lone seedpod. It was a remnant of the mangrove-lined canals and creeks that once made up Sarasota Bay before the greedy developers destroyed the once-pristine bays and estuaries. Years later, it wasn't that easy to find the seawall buried behind a jungle of red mangroves, much less find the dock. But Mother Nature found a way to hang on in a hostile environment and still thrive. "Nature always bats last," Gary Snyder echoed Robert Pyle.

I always carried a cooler full of ham sandwiches, a bag of Doritos, and a half dozen diet sodas. I could eat when I wanted to, fish when I wanted to, and come and go as I pleased without asking anyone else's permission. I was the master and commander of my seventeen-foot aluminum canoe. Eventually, the pace started to slow, the days began to lengthen, and before I knew it, I was back at the dock behind our house. By midweek, I didn't have a problem in the world. I knew the tides would shift the next day, and I would have a strong incoming tide. I wanted to jig for pompano in Big Pass for a few hours and then move up to the mouth of the pass and try to catch a few dozen mangrove snapper for dinner that night. It was amazing how many big mangrove snapper, striped grunts, and sheepshead you could catch in a good morning from the rocks at the mouth of the pass.

The beach had so little development in those days, you could pull off the road and fish almost anywhere. Fast-forward forty years, and Siesta Key has turned into a zoo. The traffic during the season is unbearable, and abundant parking has all but disappeared, all in the name of growth and development. It was Ed Abbey's iconic definition of the ideology of the cancer cell. Abbey could always be counted on to turn a phrase and piss off the right people simultaneously.

If the tide was right and the water was clean, Big Pass was the perfect place to ambush the enormous schools of pompano as they made their way into Sarasota Bay. It didn't matter which coast you lived on: if you wanted to catch pompano, March and April were your best chance. By May, the majority of migratory fish had already started their march north. Mother Nature rarely stands still for anyone, much less fishermen. That's what I always thought fishing was about, understanding all the variables and patterns in nature—letting the ebb and flow of the natural world permeate you. All good fishermen intuitively seem to understand that.

I'm not saying you can't find pompano year-round—because you can. The passes carry a few pompano throughout the year, especially if enough sand fleas and shrimp are around. You can find pompano in the bay skipping on the grass flats in the good years. It's the perfect time to drag out the fly rod. If you have the time and patience, you can also get them to hit flies in the surf. It works best on an incoming tide, especially if plenty of sand fleas are still around. Believe it or not, I knew fly fishermen who tied flies that mimicked sand fleas.

The snook had moved out of the backcountry early that year. They were starting to congregate in the mouths of the passes. The first morning I managed to hook and land two nice snook on a white bucktail and one on the fly using a small chartreuse and white Clouser Minnow with lead eyes. When I finally made it back to the house, I called Ray and told him about the snook and all the bait. He called in sick the next day and planned to meet me at the mouth of Big Pass.

I left the house a half hour before the sun was up. I was hoping to whack a few snook before Ray even crawled out of bed. It was still dark when I arrived, so I had to fish plugs until the arc of the sun was high enough to see the bait and, eventually, the snook. I walked the beach for more than an hour. Not only did I not get a hit, but the bait had disappeared, taking the snook with them. At some level I knew this would happen.

Ray thought I was lying to him, but that's fishing. Fishing is not an exact science, and it's not necessarily about catching fish; it's about the process, the craft, and your ability to understand nature. Most of all, it's about the enjoyment that fishing brings to your life. On the other hand, catching fish is your reward for spending so much time on the water and improving your skills. The more time you spend on the water, the more fish you will catch. It's been my experience that most people live their lives by the lowest common denominator, or what my close friend Doug McNair calls "living the life of least resistance."

The following day, I knew the beaches would be loaded with bait. Call it Murphy's Law of fishing. To catch fish, the one thing you have to do is fish. You have to be on the water. Unfortunately, most people would rather talk about fishing than spend the long hours needed to catch a quality fish. I didn't find much in the pass the next morning because the bait had moved out. A few hours later, I finally found the bait on the front side of the beach farther south. By the time I reached it, the blitz was in full swing. Jacks and ladyfish were everywhere. Even though I couldn't see any snook, I intuitively knew they were there somewhere, but what caught my eye were the mackerel skyrocketing through the schools of pilchards. It was a beautiful spring morning. The water was flat as glass—it mirrored the faint pink and purple thunderheads offshore. The sun was to my back, just high enough to provide an excellent view of everything happening in the water. The best part was that I had it all to myself.

The mackerel were rocketing four or five feet out of the water. I grabbed my spinning rod, put on a small croc, waded out up to my thighs, started casting over the bait, let the croc sink to the bottom, and reel as fast as possible. Usually, I would get slammed on the first drop, but if I didn't, I would repeat the process until I was either cut off or managed to hook up. I love catching mackerel and eating fresh mackerel. I probably took a dozen fish or so home that morning. I also went through every croc in my bag, and considering the cost of a new croc, other than the joy of catching a few mackerel, that morning probably cost me thirty dollars. Later that day, I cleaned the mackerel, stoked the smoker (an old gutted refrigerator I had previously converted) for an hour or so, then carefully laid in the fish. That evening, I would be fishing the bridges with Dick and the boys in the band. I knew it would only take a few minutes to go through the smoked mackerel, and with luck, someone would have a few cold beers stashed on ice in the back of their truck.

The next morning Dick and I took the back way home. I decided that it was time to check out some of the old roads that paralleled Roberts Bay and see what kind of access was available. I loved wading the grass flats, and I was always trying to get into difficult places that were traditionally off-limits. Compared to the ocean side, the bayside of Siesta Key wasn't that developed. From what I could see, some of the smaller bays and creeks could be fished on low tide or at the beginning of the incoming tide. So far, I hadn't paddled this far north, but if I played the tides right, I essentially could let the tides do all the work. As we turned the corner and headed north to Roberts Bay, I got faint whiffs of slow-burning wood and salty fish.

· 34 ·

The Plight of the Commercial Fisherman

Hang On to Your Seat

I had smelled that same aroma several times during the last few weeks, especially when the wind was blowing from the north, like the local fish market on steroids. Dick turned and looked at me, then asked if I was in the mood for some smoked mullet or maybe smoked mullet dip and crackers.

I think it took me every bit of two seconds to say yes.

We turned toward the bay down an old beat-up road smothered in spent oyster shells. The smell was horrendous. It was hard to see ten feet in front of you for the swarming flies. Finally, the road opened up to the bay surrounded by a vast mangrove estuary. I was salivating when Dick finally pulled the Ford Maverick up to the dock. I almost tripped and fell on the ground trying to get out of the car.

The little shack was nothing more than a screened porch with a half dozen picnic tables pretending to be a restaurant. The tables were covered with cheap plastic red-and-white checked tablecloths. It didn't matter which way you turned. A poor mounted fish hung on every wall, some so old and dried out that they looked pathetic. A haggard tarpon hanging over the front door was in such bad shape that it looked like it might have been caught and mounted at the turn of the century. The scales were falling off, the once translucent glass eyes had faded, and the wooden fins were hanging on by a few tattered threads. When the time comes, I hope I fare better than the tarpon.

The shack was mainly a fish market; the restaurant looked more like an afterthought. It was owned and run by the same commercial fishermen who owned all the commercial boats that lined the docks. The assortment of fish to choose from was astonishing: if the weather cooperated, the red and black grouper, mutton snapper, amberjack, and cobia came directly from the ocean the night before. The mullet fishermen and the stone crabbers hung out at the mouth of the pass, and the shrimpers stayed close to home and dredged the grass flats in Sarasota Bay.

Stone crab traps were stacked everywhere: along the docks and the sidewalks, in the parking lot, hundreds of them in every nook and cranny you could find. It didn't matter which way I looked—mullet skiffs were tied up to every conceivable dock, telephone pole, or fallen tree limbs stacked three deep. But, of course, that didn't include the six or seven boats in the workshop under construction, or being waterproofed or painted. Off to the east, several larger boats rigged for stone crabs and a few even larger trawlers were anchored in the channel.

For a minute, I thought they were part of the fleet I had seen the previous year, lined up along the Intracoastal Waterway in Fort Myers. The look and feel of the place reminded me of some of the commercial fishing villages in Chokoloskee and Everglades City, like a modern-day pirate hideout buried deep in the Ten Thousand Islands. The only thing missing was a Jolly Roger blowing in the wind from the mast of the larger trawlers. What kid wouldn't fall in love with a place like this?

A powerful fan above the entrance blew my hat off when we tried to walk through the screen door. It was amazing how much air the fan could produce! When you consider the number of flies, it couldn't blow hard enough. I couldn't believe how many of the commercial fishermen Dick knew. Of course, Dick was born and raised in Sarasota, and considering that he had been a commercial fisherman at one time, I guess it made perfect sense, especially for someone who professes to hate being on the water.

Dick's life was one long list of contradictions. Dick ran away from home and joined Ringling Bros. and Barnum & Bailey so he didn't have to work for his father and could spend more time fishing. Unfortunately, he didn't understand that the circus was always on the move, and for the next three years, he never managed to find the time to go fishing. Dick became a commercial fisherman in spite of the fact that he gets sick in the bathtub.

Other than the white rubber boots everyone wore, Dick could still pass for a commercial fisherman. I am not sure he ever changed his attire—then again, I think it was by choice. Years came and went, but Dick always looked the same. I can only assume that Mother bought him new clothes every few years. It wasn't easy to tell whether Dick had on new clothes or Mother had just washed the old ones. He always wore a dark blue short-sleeve work shirt, a black cowboy belt, and a pair of heavy-duty blue jeans held up by a pair of red suspenders. Although the cowboy hat changed throughout the years, it didn't have anything to do with taste. The old hat just disintegrated straw by straw until it fell apart.

At one time, Dick owned a mullet skiff, and to hear him tell it, he spent a small fortune on dozens of nets in multiple sizes and shapes. I should have introduced him to Frank the Net, then just stood back and watched the fireworks. Then again, they might have established a beautiful friendship that lasted the remainder of their lives. They were two different people, yet they both led very similar melancholy lives. The one thing I do know about Dick and Frank is that both of them lived life on their terms.

Dick was having a good time, and that's all that counted. You could tell that he belonged here. This was a side of Dick I had never seen before. I was ordering smoked mullet and fries; when I turned around, I saw Dick sitting on the edge of one of the picnic tables, holding court. Friends of his I had never met or even knew existed surrounded him as if they were hanging on his every word. It was different than Hart's Landing in so many ways, and I think if Old Man Hart were still alive, he would be sitting next to Dick laughing his ass off. I tried to pay for my food, and the lady behind the counter asked me if I was with Dick. When I said, "Yes," she wadded up the ticket and threw it in the trash can.

It was still relatively early in the morning, and everyone except me was drinking beer and having a wonderful time. Some were dragging nets off the boats and stretching them out over sawhorses to dry. Other fishermen were repairing what looked like seine nets used to drag the grass flats for shrimp and pass crabs, and sometimes pinfish, to sell to the bait and tackle shops. The majority of the fishermen and their kids were either repairing the stone crab traps or building new ones. Others were washing down the boats or stretching running lines for the next night. Most commercial fishing in South Florida happens at night, especially for mullet. It was a world I didn't belong to, but on some level I loved the fishermen and their families. The majority of their families went back five and six generations. I had never met anyone, much less any group of people who had so much invested in their family heritage.

The life of the commercial fishermen was difficult. It was full of rewards that few people would or could understand, which is strange because they provided a resource that came to the table through hard work. I don't think the average person understands just how much effort it takes to supply restaurants and grocery stores with fresh fish, shrimp, and crabs, not to mention oysters, clams, mussels, and live lobsters. Before they could turn a profit, they had to cover their overhead. Most commercial fishermen build their boats, especially the smaller mullet boats. Then there's the $20,000 motor attached to the transom of most mullet boats. Who knows what the big trawlers cost or what it must cost to keep everything running? I can't even imagine the size of their monthly fuel bill.

Most commercial fishermen I've met either own their property outright, or their property's mortgaged to the hilt, or some variation on the theme. Like most families, they have kids to raise, send to school, and need transportation just like you and me. They are self-employed, so they have to pay for their medical insurance, car insurance, and homeowner's insurance. Yet, their livelihood depends on the rhythm of the seasons, the abundance of fish, and the cooperation of the weather. They don't do this to get rich, and yes, they could work other jobs to make a better living. They do this because they love the freedom of the open seas, they love to fish, and they despise working for someone else. They can't fathom punching a time clock. Most of all, I think they do this because they love each other. It's not strange, considering that they live in very tight communities, and they seem to be related. Of course, they have daily arguments, and knock-down, drag-out fights once in a while, but why should they be any different than any other American family?

At some point, we need to face facts. For various reasons, some people are no longer physically or mentally capable of feeding themselves. They're addicted to the service industry, and they expect someone else to do all the work. Then the commercial fishermen have to listen to people moan and bitch about the price of fish. What would the world do without commercial fishermen? Of course, you could make the same argument for mom-and-pop farmers. For the most part, the American farmers are not doing significantly better than commercial fishermen.

You have to ask yourself, why get so fixated on the smaller things, including the local commercial fishermen, and allow the mammoth fishing fleets of the world using sophisticated satellite imagery to track and catch tens of thousands of pounds of fish a day? They process the fish at sea before they offload the catch onto smaller boats, then take it back to China, Russia, Japan, and other Asian ports. We should be talking about them and the multitude of other catastrophes that take place every day somewhere on the planet. Take, for example, the whales killed in the name of scientific research by Japan every year.

If that doesn't infuriate you, what about the invasive fish coming in on foreign tankers that continually get distributed through the watersheds? Yet, we still pick on mom-and-pop commercial fishermen and give other countries a free pass. The idea that hundreds of industrial fish farms throughout the world continually pollute the oceans and dilute the distribution of native fish without fear of retribution from the world community is deplorable. Leaving the hydroelectric dams that choke off our western rivers and prevent incredible numbers of anadromous fish from spawning in their native rivers is criminal.

The sugar industry in Florida continually pumps runoff into Lake Okeechobee, which makes its way down the Caloosahatchee River to Charlotte Harbor. Then it pollutes the harbor to the point where it's no longer suitable for life. The citrus industry has been pumping herbicides, pesticides, insecticides, and fertilizers back into the watersheds since the turn of the last century. The phosphate industry, which has been raping Florida since the late 1800s, has done more damage to South Florida than anything Mother Nature could have dreamed up.

Why do we allow companies to continue using plastic that either ends up in our land fills or in our oceans, not to mention the massive incinerators that line the East Coast and spew heavy metals across the Everglades twenty-four hours a day merely to stay in business? If you ever wonder why you can no longer eat the fish from the Everglades, you don't have to look any farther than Dade and Broward Counties. For some reason, it doesn't seem to bother too many people, but at some point you have to realize that the heavy metals poisoning the fish in the Everglades, and affecting all the wildlife there, are also raining down on you and your children.

I have no real idea what the carrying capacity of the state of Florida is. That question should be answered by a theoretical biologist, if there is such a being, but I do know that more than twenty-five million people live in Florida. More than fourteen million cars and trucks are on the highways at any one time, and more than 126 million tourists visited Florida last year. Now, can someone tell me why the mom-and-pop commercial fishermen were such a threat to the environment? Instead of fixing the big problems, Florida did everything possible to get rid of the lowest common denominator—the commercial fisherman. To find out why these things happen, just follow the money. It's been my experience that there is no such thing as the trickle-down effect, but I do believe there is a trickle-up effect. And more often than not, a politician is sitting at the top of the pyramid with his hand out.

When the opportunity to wipe out the commercial fishing industry first presented itself to the people of Florida in 1995, they jumped at it with little hesitation. Most of them knew nothing about the commercial fishing industry, or the fishermen and their families. They blindly showed up in unprecedented numbers to support putting an end to practically all commercial fishing in the state. It was simply a land grab perpetrated by corrupt politicians and land developers. The politicians in Tallahassee jumped at the opportunity to help the developers steal the majority of the commercial fishing villages in Florida in the name of conservation.

Yet, a few years later, the same people who put an end to commercial fishing had an opportunity to buy out the sugar cane industry and restore the Everglades. All they had to do was agree to a referendum proposed by the majority of environmentalists in the state to pay an additional two-cent tax on sugar. They voted it down overwhelmingly. This time it wasn't the politicians who stabbed Florida in the back. It was the people, who have always voted in favor of growth and development, and essentially been responsible for overpopulation of the state and destruction of the landscape.

The net ban eventually passed in 1995. It could have been prevented if the politicians in Tallahassee had enforced the laws already on the books. They put their hands on the Bible and swore to uphold the laws of the state. I can only assume that a lot of palms got greased that year. Florida has always been at war with itself. When you mix corrupt politicians with domestic terrorists, aka developers, and then expect an uninformed public to hold them accountable, the environment rarely wins. You can't hold the government responsible unless you understand the problems. The people have to have some skin in the game in order to make better decisions.

It was due to a combination of the state not enforcing the existing laws, and the greed and excess of the commercial fishing industry. The first thing the state needed to do was prevent commercial fishermen from other states including Georgia, South Carolina, and Alabama from setting up camp and fishing commercially in Florida waters. Second, they could have shut down various fisheries during the spawning season. Mullet traditionally spawn from November through January. The idea of netting mullet during the spawning season is absolutely absurd.

The concept of harvesting any species during spawning season is unfathomable, and yet that's what the geniuses in Tallahassee let the commercial fishermen do. Quite frankly, the average politician couldn't tell the difference between a blowfish and a tarpon. The problem is that they weren't thinking about the commercial fishing industry or the health and welfare of the state's marine fisheries. For sure they weren't thinking about the loss of biodiversity. They were thinking about lining their pockets.

Where was the Game and Fish Commission, where were the universities' marine biology and oceanography departments, where were the marine research facilities? Why didn't the public ask questions? Instead, they bought into the propaganda without thinking. It was the greedy leading the blind. The commercial fishermen were like everyone else. They had the opportunity to make a lot of money in a short period of time, and they took advantage of the loopholes in the system. You don't have to look any further than the South Florida Water District.

The commercial fishing industry virtually destroyed its own future by netting the mullet during the spawning season. The fishermen were making a tremendous amount of money from the mullet roe, much more than they could ever make off of mullet itself. The Japanese were buying as much mullet roe as they could get their hands on and paying the fishermen exorbitant prices for it. In the end, the commercial fishermen were harvesting the roe; there wasn't much demand for the mullet, so they threw the dead mullet back into the water.

They were worse than a bunch of drunken tourists on a winning spree at the blackjack table in Vegas. It went on for years, and every year saw fewer and fewer mullet. They never took the time to think about what would happen when the fish disappeared. The money was intoxicating, and a few years later, the mullet were all but gone. Twenty-five years later, the mullet runs are a mere shadow of their former glory. When the net ban passed in 1995, the commercial fishermen had to sell their boats and nets to the state of Florida. Eventually, the properties their families had lived on and fished for generations went to developers, nothing more than modern-day carpetbaggers.

In the end, the commercial fishermen lost the battle. Still, the people who voted for the net ban suffered the most, though I doubt if anyone cared or understood what had happened. The loss of cultural diversity was staggering. The culture and the history of generations of commercial fishermen and their families have all but faded away. At some level, it's gut wrenching, at least from my perspective. The loss of cultural diversity is every bit as important as the loss of biodiversity in the South. In some ways, cultural diversity and biodiversity are joined at the hip, impossible to separate, although I don't think it ever occurred to the people who now call Florida home. The developers and the politicians won again.

I still fish places such as Sanibel and Naples throughout the summer and fall for snook, and from what I have seen of the net ban, it hasn't made the fisheries any better. Compared to the environmental disasters of the past few years, the commercial fishing industry was relatively harmless. The question is, how long will the United States continue to let foreign countries decimate our fisheries?

The same thing is happening to the stone crab industry. From what I have seen and what commercial fishermen have told me, the Japanese meet the commercial stone crabbers at the docks and buy the majority of stone crab claws long before they make it to market. And when stone crab claws make it to the market, the prices are insane for the crab claws that the Japanese didn't want in the first place. That alone should give you pause before you cough up $45 a pound for rejects.

The same thing is happening off the northeast coast with the Atlantic bluefin tuna. Bluefin tuna goes for about $40 a pound at the docks. Recently I read where a 608-pound tuna went for $1,800,000 at auction in Japan. Meanwhile, the bluefin tuna population is disappearing at an alarming rate. If something doesn't change quickly, the bluefin tuna will eventually disappear altogether. China and Japan are emptying the oceans at an alarming rate. And instead of stopping the mass slaughter of all the marine species on the planet, we help them—or at the very least, turn our backs to what's happening. It speaks volumes about the priorities of the human race.

We have long passed the point of no return. The environment will never be better than it is today. The fishing will never be remotely close to what I experienced growing up in South Florida, the once light tackle capital of the world. When I think about it, I get depressed. I want to shut out the world and do my best to ignore what's been happening for the past several hundred years.

And yet, I can run into a young kid on the beach with a new fly rod, and he's completely oblivious to what has happened to his fishery over the past fifty or sixty years. All he is interested in is catching a few fish to take home for dinner. Maybe it's supposed to be that way. Perhaps fishing is really meant for kids. Who knows? Maybe at some point, we're supposed to stop fishing and move on to more important things, golf or tennis.

• *35* •

A Time to Remember

$\mathscr{T}$he day was May 25, 1973. It was a Saturday morning, and I had an appointment to take my driving test at the Florida Department of Motor Vehicles in the Gulf Gate Mall at ten-thirty that morning. I was anything but nervous. My mother, on the other hand, was scared to death. It took her three tries to pass the parallel parking part. My mother wasn't worried that I wouldn't pass the written portion of the driver's exam, but she was convinced I would flunk the driving test. I tried to tell her that I had been backing boat trailers in and out of the water for several years. Parallel parking couldn't be that hard. Even Ralph trusted me to back his skiff down some of the worst ramps in Broward County.

I wanted to show up in Ray's old truck, if nothing else to see the look on the driving instructor's face. But of course, my mother didn't want any part of it. I never knew if she didn't want to be seen in Ray's truck, or if she was terrified of what the instructor might assume, or worse might do, when he saw that rundown piece of junk. I breezed through the parallel parking without a hiccup. At least, that was my first impression.

The instructor knew I could parallel park long before he climbed into the car. When the driving test was over, he hinted that I might want to slow down the next time and pay more attention to what I was doing—and look in both directions the next time I tried to parallel park. He tried his best not to laugh; he just smiled and walked away. I never had the heart to tell my mother he was one of my football coaches—and my driver's education instructor.

When we made it back to the house, a red 1969 Ford Bronco was sitting in the driveway along with a half dozen other cars and trucks. I asked my mother what was happening. She merely shrugged her shoulders and said she didn't have any idea. I kept telling myself that was a stupid answer, but there wasn't much else she could say.

When I walked through the door, virtually everyone I knew was there. I had to act excited, mesmerized, and stunned. But how did I know how to act? In sixteen years, it was my first real birthday party. I recognized almost all of the cars in our driveway except the Ford Bronco. Harold and Sarah were there, and of course, Dick; the first car I saw was his rundown Ford Maverick. It would have stuck out like a sore thumb if Ray's old orange Florida Power and Light truck hadn't been parked next to it. Together they constituted a miniature junkyard.

My parents were grilling ribs and burgers on the back porch. It was the first time I had seen my mother and stepfather grill anything together. My stepfather was a good cook, and for the most part, when he wasn't working, he usually did the cooking. More often than not, my mother's idea of dinner came out of a box and took only minutes to cook. Once she discovered the microwave, she never took time to prepare a normal dinner again. After dinner, I started opening my birthday gifts very slowly; I wanted to savor the experience. Not to make too big a deal about it, but it was a pretty good haul.

I usually got a birthday card with a few bucks and twenty or thirty McDonald's gift certificates, and that was about it. I did get a card from my father that had a considerable amount of money in it and an insurance card made out to me for a 1969 Ford Bronco. My father usually sent me a few bucks on my birthday, although he refused to pay my mother child support or alimony because she had quickly remarried. I didn't say anything until I knew for sure, but I figured out the Bronco had to be my birthday present from him.

Just how liberating my sixteenth birthday was is almost impossible to describe. My world changed overnight, and my options were virtually limitless.

I could have loaded at least some of my fishing gear and a few surfboards in the Bronco and headed to Fort Lauderdale that night for all practical purposes. Four or five hours later, I could have been fishing at Anglin's Pier. I could have taken Ralph and Linda up on their offer to move in with them. It was touch-and-go for the next several hours. It's hard to describe how tempting Ralph and Linda's offer was and how much I wanted to accept it. But I needed to find another job and finish school as soon as possible. I needed to make and save as much money as I could over the next eighteen months.

By this time, I had already worked for my stepfather part-time for several years. I was working in the kitchen three, sometimes four nights a week. Other weeks I didn't get to work at all. If someone didn't show up, or an employee needed to take time off, I was always available for the right price. It didn't matter to me: work was work, and I needed the money. I worked as a line cook, prep cook, and sometimes a dishwasher.

Over the last several years, I must have shucked tens of thousands of oysters and peeled two or three trawl nets full of shrimp. I cleaned up at night; on more than one occasion, I had to clean out the dumpsters and take out the trash. I worked as a waiter more often than I like to admit. The outfit I had to wear was embarrassing: who wants to wear a bow tie? The name of the restaurant was embarrassing enough. Everything about Happy Land Seafood was a little over the top, but night after night, tourists showed up in huge numbers, and on the weekend, a long line was always waiting at the door. I was always afraid someone from school would see me in that stupid outfit; the only reason I tolerated it was that the tips were great. I'm still amazed at how much crap you're willing to put up with when you are a kid. Nothing seems to bother you as long as you're getting paid. Getting paid off the books was even better. I still needed to find another part-time job to supplement what I was making working for my stepfather.

If nothing else, I could pick up a few hours at the surf shop. But the shop was selling more than surfboards in those days, and I knew, sooner or later, it would come crashing down, and I didn't want to be there when it happened. I always thought my mother suspected me of smoking pot. I didn't. But my clothes must have reeked of it—I was in the shop so often my hair, even my skin, must have smelled like weed. It was about that time I first heard the phrase "secondhand buzz." I'm still not sure I believe it, but denial is the first indication that you are a user.

Several weeks later, I strolled into the Pizza Hut located a few hundred yards down the road from Economy Tackle to apply for a job. A Pizza Hut, a Mister Donut, and Lums Restaurant faced each other on US 41. I loved pizza, so I initially chose Pizza Hut. If I didn't get the job, I would apply to Lums next; and if that didn't work out, Mister Donut awaited. I struck gold! The manager was a twenty-six-year-old hippie named Martin. He had just transferred to Sarasota from Lake Worth, and he loved to fish. And like me, he grew up on a fishing pier.

After I filled out the application, he smiled and stuffed it in a drawer. I doubt he ever looked at it again. It was almost an instantaneous friendship. It was still several hours before the store opened, so he cranked up the pizza oven and tossed in a massive thin and crispy meat lover's delight. We sat around and ate pizza for the next several hours and told fishing stories. Employees began drifting in one by one and started prepping their stations. Martin kept asking me when I could start; the next day after school was it. Only a few weeks of school were left, and I could work more hours during the summer. I did everything to talk my way out of working on weekends, and to some extent, it worked. I rarely had to work on Friday and Saturday nights. Martin handed me three new Pizza Hut shirts and a couple of hats. As I was walking out the door, I asked him about the pay. With a smile, he said, "Two dollars and sixty-five cents an hour." I smiled back and left, wondering whether that was a lot.

Between Pizza Hut and Happy Land, I worked around twenty hours a week; to be honest, I was making exponentially more money working at Happy Land. I hung in there for the next six or seven months, but it was useless. I didn't have much free time between Happy Land and spring training. Then, when school started, I had football practice after school, which virtually eliminated all my free time.

Until my birthday, I didn't have any transportation except for my bicycle. I had to depend on friends for a ride, fishing when and where they wanted to fish. I wanted to try some of the more famous bridges north of Sarasota, especially the New Pass Bridge. Dick and Lew gave me fair warning: stay away on the weekends because of the massive crowds. The bridge is so popular with local snook fishermen that parents would drop their kids off early to stake out the best possible spots.

Some families stayed the entire weekend to avoid losing their place on the bridge. I had seen the same thing the first time I fished Sebastian Inlet. Fishermen lined the catwalk shoulder to shoulder. The catwalks were often tricky to navigate, and finding a decent place to fish was ridiculous. If the fishing was hot, it was almost unbearable. I would like to tell you that everybody knew what they were doing, but sadly they didn't. For the most part, good fishermen wouldn't be caught dead there.

If New Pass was really that good, why not fish it during the week? That left Dick out because of his deal with Mother. Theirs was an ironclad agreement, and the last thing Dick wanted was to tempt providence. I grabbed a few rods and a lantern late Wednesday night and drove to the bridge. I had the perfect tide. By the time I got there, I figured the tide would be slack, and by the time I had everything set up, the incoming tide should be building up steam. Unfortunately, when I arrived at the bridge, people were stacked two deep on the west side facing the incoming tide. It was a madhouse.

If I wasn't tripping over the fishing rods, I was tripping over lawn chairs. Everybody had an ice chest, some idiots had two, and almost everyone had a live well. It reminded me of crazy tailgating parties at the Orange Bowl I took part in before a Dolphins game.

I turned around and started working my way back down the bridge. Then I spotted the boats anchored at the mouth of the pass. It was one boat short of Boca Grande pass during tarpon season. When I finally found a place to peek over the railing, I did see tons of bait, and snook were stacked like cordwood. Three or four boats were fishing the light at the end of the fender. The one thing I didn't see was snook coming over the railings. In the end, I should have heeded Dick and Lew's warning and stayed away.

A few weeks later, I drove over the bridge on an outgoing tide and didn't see many people fishing. I didn't take time to stop and fish the east side of the bridge. But tons of shrimp probably were floating out with the tide, and from what I knew about snook, I can't believe they weren't stacked in the channel, crushing the shrimp. I have seen several bridges over the years that fished great on one tide, and when it changed direction, the snook completely disappeared.

• 36 •

Myakka State Park

The Crappie Capital of the World

$\mathscr{M}$yakka State Park was gorgeous when I first fished it, and from what I have been told, it's still as beautiful as the day I first dipped my paddle in the river. The Myakka River flowed down from the north through Manatee County and snaked its way through some of the best bottomland left in Florida.

It was almost prehistoric. Herds of wild hogs rooted around in the mud and mucked along the banks in the early morning. Even though they wreaked havoc with the native plants and small grubs that lived in the soil, they were fun to watch. As the sun peeked over the horizon, the gators began dragging their massive bodies up on the beach to take advantage of the warming sun. Flora and fauna inside the park were still intact in the early seventies. The *Sarasota Herald-Tribune* once referred to the upper river as the last remnant of the Garden of Eden.

Most of the river north of the park was in private hands, and if you knew the right people, you could get access to float the river as long as you didn't pull out and camp. Originally, the Myakka River flowed uninterrupted down to Charlotte Harbor. In the early 1800s, a Seminole supposedly once told a trapper that the river's name was the Myakka, and the name stuck.

The water flows freely over the weir and then south into the lower lake during the summer. From what I can tell, the lower lake is nothing more than a series of deep sinkholes created by the porous limestone. The river eventually changes direction several times, twisting and turning as the water makes its way south. I haven't floated the Myakka in years. But the people who still take care of the park tell me the river still flows south without interruption until it dumps into Charlotte Harbor.

The fishing in the park was outstanding and still is. The park has always had an excellent largemouth bass fishery, but I spent most of my free time fishing for crappie through the winter months. When I did have time to fish the upper lake for bass, especially during the dog days of summer, the heat and humidity could be brutal. The giant thunderheads that seemed to boil up over the horizon were almost artistic. The thunder that rolled across the wiregrass prairies throughout the summer was deafening—a brutal assault on your senses.

One afternoon Ray and I were huddled under a giant oak tree smothered in Spanish moss, waiting out one of the loudest thunderstorms I had ever experienced. It was so mighty that you could feel the ground shake, rattle, roll, and then watch it vibrate across the lake. The old oak was moaning and groaning from the gale force winds as if it would split down the middle at any time. Lightning bolts struck the ground as if Ray and I had done something to offend the gods. So much static electricity was in the air; you could taste the burn. I love storms! They make me feel alive and yet so small. It's a little disconcerting to realize that control, absolute control, is nothing more than an illusion.

I know it was stupid to wait out a thunderstorm under a big oak tree, but I've done dumber things. We turned over the canoe and rode out the storm for the next thirty minutes. Storms blow through quickly in the South, and after a few minutes, they're gone. Usually, then, the water calms down, the air gets a little cooler, the humidity dials back a notch, and the fishing gets better.

In the winter months, crappie fishing is great if you can find them, and once you find them, you can spend the day within a few hundred yards from where you started. In the right place, on a good day, you could fill the cooler with white and black crappie. And if you were so inclined, you could take home a few dozen catfish if you didn't mind using frozen chicken livers for bait. It's an acquired taste. I know it sounds a little southern, but Florida has always been a southern state, if not a little redneck.

· 37 ·

Never Underestimate a Saltwater Crocodile

$\mathcal{T}$he Myakka River's mouth, where it dumps into Charlotte Harbor at El Jobean, created one of the most fertile estuaries found on the west coast. In late summer and early fall, the snook and the tarpon fishing could be phenomenal on an incoming tide. We used to call it the magic hour, the period between twilight and dark, the moment just before the sun starts to fade, the water erupts, and silver mullet explode everywhere. Vast schools of jack crevalle would invade the river mouth and feast on the mullet. The river contained so many jacks that the water had a yellow cast.

The grass flats and oyster bars were always a great place to wade and fly-fish for reds, sea trout, and the occasional snook. If you wanted to drag plastic baits slowly along the bottom, you could catch a washtub full of flounder on an incoming tide. The entire estuary at high tide was teeming with sheepshead and black drum. I've even seen a few big tripletail hanging on the ropes that anchor the crab traps during the winter. If you wanted to get your clock cleaned, all you had to do was pitch a live pinfish to one of the huge cobia that hung around the bridge pilings in the spring and hold on.

The red mangroves carpeted the mouth of the Myakka River, and thick stands of buttonwoods stood tall behind them. But if you took the time to dig deeper, you would find black mangroves deep in the estuaries. You can always tell the black mangroves by all the pneumatophores sticking up in the mud or sand, which help supply the mangroves with oxygen in submerged soils. The place was alive with dozens of species of wading birds, crabs, raccoons, the occasional alligator, and, depending on whom you believe, the rare crocodile. Every once in a while, you could see giant stingrays blowing off the flats. If you were lucky, you might see flocks of white pelicans sunning on a sandbar at low tide, or run into huge pods of manatees in the winter, trying to stay warm and chowing down on all the grass flats. If you took time to look up, you had an excellent chance of spotting a frigate bird—sometimes lots of frigate birds—soaring in giant circles, looking for God knows what.

The Myakka River watershed is enormous, and when I was growing up in the early seventies, it was still intact and thriving. At that time, places such as Englewood, Placida, El Jobean, North Port Charlotte, and Port Charlotte were nothing more than specks on the map—quaint little cities along Highway 41 that, for the most part, other than a few strip malls here and there and the occasional car dealership, were full of freshwater canals and an endless supply of bass and bluegills. It didn't take a genius to see that all this eventually would come to a halt. The population would skyrocket, the traffic would increase tenfold, and crime would multiply exponentially.

The spillway behind the Winn-Dixie in Port Charlotte was one of the best on the west coast. But unfortunately, the Southwest Florida Water Management District would fence it off to prevent fishermen from fishing there. That should have been the first sign of trouble. The west coast eventually would look more and more like the east coast, one long stretch of humanity from Tampa to Naples.

When I-75 was finished, it took some pressure off US 41, increasing the number of people wanting to move to Florida. In the early seventies, the number of people moving into the state was staggering, if not paralyzing at times. I can't blame people for wanting to move to Florida. It's the state I grew up in and a place dear to my heart.

Long before the sugar cane industry, the citrus industry, and the phosphate mines, John Kunkel Small, a botanist at Columbia University and the first curator of the museums at the New York Botanical Gardens, once called Florida the Garden of Eden. In 1929 Science Press published Small's *From Eden to Sahara*, chronicling years of devastation of the plant community throughout the south since his last visit, and in 1944 Little, Brown and Company published *That Vanishing Eden: A Naturalist's Florida* by Thomas Barbour. At some point, we have to ask ourselves, what went wrong?

About halfway from Sarasota to Myakka State Park, you crossed a drainage ditch. During the rainy season, the banks would swell, and the little ditch would be thirty or forty feet wide; depending on the amount of rain, it could be four or five feet deep. It would shrink to about ten feet wide and two or three feet deep during the winter months. It always held water, and the current varied with the seasons. Occasionally a few sandbars appeared in the middle, which created a few faster channels and undercut banks to the side. It doesn't sound important unless you like catching largemouth bass. The faster channels were always cooler and highly oxygenated. In the summer, when temperatures climbed upwards of a hundred degrees, the bass congregated in the cooler water at the tail out of the smaller channels.

If you look at a map of Sarasota and Manatee County, it seems like Cow Pen Slough comes from nowhere. It just pops up in the middle of a cow pasture and flows south. I can only assume that's why it's called Cow Pen Slough. If you follow it on the map from its origin, it eventually dumps into Shakett Creek, which empties into Donna Bay. The bay leads to the Gulf of Mexico via the Venice Jetties. Dozens of smaller tributaries flow into Cow Penn Slough along the way. The only real impediment was a relatively unknown spillway where it dumped into Shakett Creek.

The majority of the slough runs through private lands, and for all practical purposes, it's off-limits to most fishermen—at least it was in the early seventies. The only place for the public to access the slough was from Route 72. You could pull off the road beside the little bridge and fish a hundred feet north and south of the highway. If you were creative, you could float the slough from the bridge in a canoe, but you would need someone to run a shuttle. You would have to pull the canoe and portage around the spillway, drop your canoe back into Shakett Creek, and pull out at the bridge on US 41 in Nokomis. Ray and I did it many times, especially in the fall. The problem is that the people who own the property on both sides of the slough would probably make sure you never did it again.

The problem was the fishermen. For some reason, they took it upon themselves to pull out anywhere they wanted to, camp, and make a mess. If they had left the camps the way they found them, it might have been a different story. It's a sad commentary, but at one time, you could pull off the road and knock on someone's farmhouse door and ask permission to fish their farm pond or creek; more often than not, they would let you. Those days are gone forever, unless you happen to be part of the local farm community.

Sometimes it's just better to be lucky. I had friends and a few cousins twice removed who lived reasonably close to where Cow Pen Slough came out of the ground. It was nothing more than a small creek at the top. Ray also knew several families who owned property south of Route 72. Over the years, we managed to fish long sections of the slough. It mainly held bass and bluegills. The fish were primarily on the small side, but we caught a few three- or four-pound bass occasionally.

It's incredible how many of these little gems still flow through the South Florida landscape. Finding them is another story. It's not difficult, but it does require a little effort and reconnaissance work. Of course, that's only half the battle; once you find them, you still need the time and energy to explore them. Often these little jewels are hard to crack. Sadly, if you want to get away from the masses and experience what's left of old Florida, you have to get down on your hands and knees and crawl, and if you're lucky, you might find a little Shangri-la for yourself.

Then, sometimes, you find nothing more than a drainage ditch full of mosquitoes. On the other hand, you might get crushed and eaten alive by a fifteen-foot Burmese python, or better yet, you could be shredded, then eaten by a Komodo dragon. It's tough to tell sometimes. In the end, that's what life is really about for some people, unraveling the mysteries of nature, and at the same time trying to avoid getting your ass chewed off.

It makes being bitten by a six-foot rattlesnake almost seem like a pleasant experience. I would bet that being drowned by a ten-foot alligator and then stuffed under a submerged log for several weeks to soften you up doesn't sound so bad. Eventually, you have to ask yourself how many different ways can man come up with to destroy South Florida's environment? How many invasive species do we have to introduce into the landscape before we learn our lesson? How many mistakes do we have to make before we lose everything? Some might argue that we are long past that point, and the future has already been decided.

I have some news for the folks who live in North Florida. As the climate continues to warm, the seas continue to rise, the line between the subtropics and the more temperate climates of the north begins to shift, you will also get to enjoy the invasive wildlife that's slowly eating its way north. It's a sobering thought. It's almost as if we're part of a science fiction movie, and it's been my experience that the planet doesn't fare too well in most films.

The Fall Migration

It's tough to get any meaningful work done in the fall, like an itch you can't scratch. But more often than not, it's something that you feel intuitively. Everything seems to be in flux. The pilchards, threadfins, and multitudes of other whitebait were starting to show up. The birds were beginning to migrate south in huge numbers. The fall mullet run was underway, the snook were fattening up for the winter months, and the temperatures were dropping.

If you lived in North Florida, the trees would change colors and eventually lose their leaves. Not in South Florida. The only way to tell the difference between late summer and early fall is the subtle migration of the bait and birds heading south. It's the subtle differences in nature that people lose sight of, like the minute difference between fishing and catching.

The fall semester had been underway for a few months, and I knew that I needed to bear down and study. I was so far behind. I was beginning to believe it would be impossible to catch up. I was failing most of my classes, football was underway, and somewhere in the middle of this chaos, I managed to find a new girlfriend. To make things a little more complicated, I worked four or five nights a week for my stepfather. For the first time in my life, I was only fishing one or two nights a week.

After I finished work on Saturday night, I always met Dick and the boys on a bridge somewhere to do something—if nothing else, drink coffee and catch up. Sometimes we ended up at Hart's Landing on Sunday morning, just in time to snag a few doughnuts before they were gone. Then we would sit around and tell lies. Try to explain that one to a new girlfriend! It reminded me of the big hit by Willie Nelson and Waylon Jennings, "Mammas Don't Let Your Babies Grow Up to Be Cowboys."

All I needed to do was replace cowboys with fishermen.

It's incredible, and sometimes appropriate, that life can be summed up neatly in the lyrics of a great country and western song. It reminds me of the phrase Harlan Howard coined in the early fifties, describing the similarities between country and western music and life: "All I got is a red guitar, three chords, and the truth."

If that doesn't sum up life, I don't know what does.

A few weeks later, I was looking for a new girlfriend. It wasn't my first breakup, but it was undoubtedly the fastest. Face it: being a teenager is painful enough, sometimes unbearable, but if you don't take care of the tiny bumps in the road quickly, they can turn into mountains, and then your life starts to unravel. It's not the end of the world. It's just a problem that needs to be solved. Years later, I learned that life's most challenging issues usually exist between your ears.

All I had to do was slow down and study more, and it probably wouldn't have hurt if I had started attending class once in a while. But I still had things I wanted to do and places I wanted to fish by the end of the year, and none of them had anything to do with school.

Even on the east coast, the Green Bridge in Bradenton was legendary. I kept hearing incredible stories from other fishermen about gargantuan snook that moved into the Manatee River during the winter months. I was going to fish the Green Bridge this year, even if I had to skip school. I still wanted to float the Peace River in March and April outside of Arcadia for snook and tarpon. Ray and I still needed to fish his secret lake south of Englewood. Frank kept promising to take me down to Port Charlotte to fish the spillway behind the Winn-Dixie.

I still had so many places to explore and not enough time to fish them all. I was only sixteen years old, but at some level, I understood what that meant, and the last thing on my mind was compromising. Yet, life, for the most part, is about compromise. I spent the Thanksgiving holidays in the public library catching up and studying for finals. I spent the entire Christmas holiday getting a jump on spring semester. I wanted to spend as much time as possible fishing the Green Bridge in January and February.

If I worked hard and kept my nose to the grindstone, I could float the Peace River in March over spring break. Of course, it would be a logistical nightmare, but at least I had a blueprint. I remember the first time Ray and I walked out onto the Green Bridge. It was a little after midnight, and the tide was starting to change. It was an old bridge that had seen better days, but it still had a funky appeal. And yes, the Green Bridge was green! There wasn't much traffic at that time of night, and from what I could see, we had the bridge to ourselves.

We knew the snook started moving into the Manatee River when the temperatures began to drop. We kept hearing stories about the herculean effort it took to land a mammoth snook. We bought into all the tales—hook, line, and sinker. I can't tell you how many times I asked Dick about the Green Bridge, and every time I asked him, he just shrugged his shoulders and repeated the same old stories. Then you show up one cold night in January, the tides are right, you have the right gear, and you even remembered to bring a six-foot bridge net, and the bridge is empty. We looked at each other as if to say, what's wrong with this picture? If this bridge is so good, why are we the only fishermen here?

There wasn't much we could do at this point. We were here to fish for snook on the legendary Green Bridge, and that's what we were going to do. The bridge had been there for a long time. I can only imagine the fish that came over the railings through the years and the stories of the fishermen who once fished it. A few big marinas were on the north and south sides of the bridge, expensive sailboats anchored in the channel, old rundown houseboats moored at the marina, and most of them seemed occupied. It wasn't precisely like Stock Island, but then again, it wasn't that different either. You could hear the occasional television, and on one of the larger houseboats, the captain was having a small dinner party on the upper deck. I have no idea why the traffic was essentially nonexistent.

The question was where to start. It would be a piece of cake; nothing to it. We talked it over for a few minutes before Ray decided he would start somewhere around the draw, and I would peddle my wares at the beginning of the bridge next to the marina. The timing was right—the tide was starting to flood—and for all practical purposes, the snook should have been there. The first problem I ran into was these giant plugs. It wasn't like pitching a jig or a small Rapala under a light somewhere. Before we left, I spooled Penn 704 with seventeen-pound test Trilene XL. I used a two-foot leader of a sixty-pound test Tournament Ande and another sixteen inches of eighty-pound test as a shock tippet. The last thing I wanted to do was lose a big snook around the bridge pilings.

It's a paradox. The boats and the pier constituted a modern-day nightmare, yet I knew they attracted the snook. Snook tend to congregate under the hulls of anchored boats during the winter months; the colder the water, the more snook and the closer to the hull they get. If the water gets too cold, they eventually get sluggish, and it's almost impossible to get them to feed. That's why they move up into the rivers. The freshwater is always a few degrees warmer than the saltwater. If the water temperature drops too much, the snook can, and often do, freeze to death.

I reared back and fired the CD-18 as far as I could. The plug almost took my head off. Then, the plug took off and never seemed to slow down. The line was disappearing off my reel at the speed of light. The heavy plug kept going, and going, and going over the top of the houseboats and finally landed somewhere in the mouth of the river. I dumped almost half my spool of line. To make things worse, I had no idea where my plug was, and I had no idea how to get it back. My line was lying over the top of a half dozen houseboats and one sailboat. Even more depressing, my fishing line was lying across the houseboat's dinner table, where they were having a quiet dinner party.

Later that night, I bounced one off the hull of a big sailboat. It made such a ruckus that half the lights in the marina came on. I knew where I wanted to fish, and I wanted to fish as close to the hulls as possible. It still didn't matter. I didn't get a single hit. For all I knew, no fish were in the river yet, but still out in the bay gorging on shrimp. Maybe the water wasn't cold enough. It takes a lifetime on the water to understand the nature of fish and their relationship with the tides and the seasons. The answers never come easily.

I was trying to tie on another plug when I heard Ray scream something from the other end of the bridge. I grabbed the net and ran as fast as possible, carrying a six-foot bridge net and dragging fifty or sixty feet of rope behind me. By the time I got to Ray, he had about a twenty-pound snook straight up and down. I had to drop the net, then have Ray slide the snook in and pull it up and over the railing. The snook was long and skinny, but she had broad shoulders. Her fins were still translucent, and her flanks were still bright silver. A few days earlier, she was probably in a pass somewhere or out front on the beaches. It was obvious she had just spawned.

Then it dawned on me that most of the snook in the river this time of year were probably spawned-out females. They were looking for warm water and something to eat. I had no idea why they were here. The beaches had plenty of bait, and the water wasn't that cold. Maybe the river was full of mullet. Years earlier, I had kept a big female I caught when I was fishing the hot water canal with Ralph; I would never kill another one unless she didn't look like she was going to survive. And after I saw what the massive treble hooks did to her mouth, I switched them for single hooks or bounced plastic baits along the bottom.

I didn't catch a snook that night, much less get a bite. And I didn't fish the Green Bridge again until twelve years later.

I couldn't get it out of my mind just how many females had been taken over the years. Every year there seemed to be fewer and fewer snook. Eventually, they had to close the spawning season altogether, though it didn't stop people from poaching snook during the closed season. That's almost unthinkable. It's a crime against nature, driven by greed, stupidity, or both. Some forty years later, fishermen are still poaching snook during the spawning season. It's repulsive and should never happen.

In the early seventies, the west coast was a mecca for snook. I would bet that we had 80, maybe 90 percent more snook than we have today. By the time I came along, we had already lost 50 percent of the fish from the previous generation. I'm amazed any snook are left. But I have to be honest: with all the growth and development, the runoff, and the pollution from the sugar and citrus industries, snook are thriving on the east coast north of Broward County, despite our best efforts to destroy the environment. The east coast has plenty of brood stock to replenish the snook population on the west coast if people would clean up the environment and restore places like Charlotte Harbor.

Florida needs to act quickly and invest in the fisheries on the west coast before it's all gone. So little is left that it's almost ridiculous to still call it a fishery. Charlotte Harbor is on the verge of collapse, and if this keeps up, the shattered fishery will be the latest environmental disaster to hit Florida. The seagrasses are almost entirely gone, the shrimp and crabs have all but disappeared, and what few trout and redfish we have left are only hatchery fish. The snook population has been decimated over the past twenty years, yet the Chamber of Commerce keeps telling everyone snook is on the rebound.

Not so. The snook have virtually disappeared. If this keeps going at the same pace, Charlotte Harbor will be a wasteland within the next ten years. I have talked to some biologists who believe Charlotte Harbor already is, though that doesn't make Charlotte Harbor unique. Most of the fisheries throughout North America are in the same sad shape. They're propped up by state and federally funded fisheries programs. You might as well be fishing at Disneyland.

The upside to having access to pristine fisheries throughout the world is that I get to enjoy what's left; the downside is that I get to see the same fisheries slowly disappear. We are losing the battle at a far faster pace than you can imagine.

• 39 •

Peace River, Myakka River, and Cow Pen Slough

$\int$pring break was right around the corner, and Ray and I were already planning to float the Peace River and try to persuade a few snook and tarpon to hit a fly. Even though I had never fished it, Ray was from Arcadia, and he grew up fishing the Peace River. He didn't remember seeing snook or tarpon, which was a little disconcerting. If nothing else, we could always fish for bass and bluegills. The float alone would be worth the trip. The section of the river south of the Lettuce Lake boat ramp had graced the covers of multiple fishing magazines. It had to be true if it made its way into *Florida Sportsman.*

The Peace River is not a place you want to fish on the weekend. The river was full of happy-go-lucky families in canoes and inner tubes, floating the river and picnicking along the banks when they could find a place to pull out. Even in the seventies, both sides of the river were still in private hands. The banks looked like I-75. Private property signs were posted every ten feet, on almost every palm tree stretched out over the river. It made the river look trashy, though I could understand their point. People have a bad habit of loving something to death.

It only took a little over an hour to get to Arcadia from Sarasota, though it seemed longer. We always had to fight the dense fog, which never seemed to disappear. It hung low to the ground, and for all we knew, it went on forever. It was a straight shot to Arcadia if you took Clark Road east. Once you left Sarasota, other than a few scattered houses, the landscape consisted of a few cow pastures, state land, Myakka River State Park, and the occasional small farm. At times, we crept along at ten miles an hour. Between the fog and the occasional gust of wind, it was challenging to keep the Bronco on the road. I was always worried about getting pancaked by a giant eighteen-wheeler barreling down the road in dense fog at sixty miles an hour. Nevertheless, the drive over and back was always interesting, regardless of the weather.

We tried our best to have the canoe in the water at first light. To do that, we had to leave Sarasota a few hours before dawn. We passed the exit to Lettuce Lake three or four times on the way over, and we passed it three or four times going in the other direction, just trying to find the turnoff.

The ride home seemed even longer. More often than not, we were fighting late afternoon thunderstorms, or at the very least, torrential downpours. We always tried to have dinner in Arcadia before heading home. It made for a long day, but it was worth it in the end. Over the next four days, we learned a lot about fly-fishing out of a canoe.

Until now, we had used the canoe primarily for transportation from one grass flat to the other. Rarely had we ever fished out of it because it was too noisy. We were constantly spooking fish off the flats. All it took was one little bump with the push pole, and the fish scattered like someone had thrown a cherry bomb in the water. An aluminum canoe has advantages, but stealth is not one.

It didn't take long to figure out that two people can't fly-fish out of the same canoe simultaneously, especially if the fisherman in front is standing up. The fisherman in the stern needs to be both master and commander, and be willing to cater to the fisherman in front. He needs to keep the canoe in position, drop and raise the anchor, control the speed of the drift, and pretty much play guide. Most of all, he needs to remember that sooner or later, he will swap positions, and what's good for the goose is good for the gander.

We always carried a few extra spinning rods and a couple of baitcasting rods so the fisherman in the back could fish. Normally, the fisherman in the stern outfished the poor guy standing up pitching flies. Depending on how well the two fishermen know each other, it can be a touchy situation. Sometimes the fisherman in the back should take the high road and stop fishing, but that rarely happens, and in Ray's case, never. So, you had to keep one eye on the fish and one eye on Ray at all times.

It's amazing how productive a small black and gold Rapala can be on small rivers. Bass, snook, and even small tarpon love them. It doesn't matter if you're fishing the Peace River, Myakka River, or the Cow Pen Slough. The trick is to match the hatch, and that means the color and the size of the bait. At times, small rivers can be somewhat tannic, and the water looks dark. Don't be fooled by the apparent color of the water. It can be clear, but the bottom of the river can be covered in brown algae and smothered by organic litter, such as decomposing leaves or other compost. It gives the illusion that the water's stained. Most of the bait in the river will be painted in dark browns, motor oils, and variations of yellows and dark greens. The fish are sporting a complex mixture of earth tones.

Canoes are great. I love them, but they have their limitations. The biggest downside to a canoe is the long paddle back to the boat ramp. On the first day, we must have floated three or four miles before we realized that we would have to paddle back against the current at day's end. We were lucky that the Peace River was relatively low, considering the amount of rain we had gotten for several days. On the first day, we caught seven small snook and jumped three or four baby tarpon. We also caught dozens of one- or two-pound bass and accidentally hooked two small alligators from the back of the canoe. Most of the tarpon were between ten and twelve pounds. Ray managed to hook one tarpon somewhere around thirty pounds, but the fight only lasted for a few seconds. After three jumps, the tarpon just laughed and headed south, taking Ray's Rapala with him.

Most of the fish came from the undercut banks where the water was deeper and seemed to run faster. The Peace River wasn't very wide around Arcadia. It was relatively small and easy to fish. The snook looked like they had been in the freshwater for a long time. Their flanks were a combination of deep bronze and a butterscotch yellow, and their fins were no longer translucent but dark black. I have no idea why they were here. It's about forty miles from Arcadia to Charlotte Harbor as the crow flies; that's not that far for snook or tarpon to migrate, but I find it hard to believe that any of these fish had ever seen the salt. Even the tarpon had a dark bronze tint to them. The Game and Fish Commission once told me that the snook and tarpon in the Peace River tend to disappear after the second or third week of April. I always wanted to know why and, if so, where did they go? It seemed like an honest question, but I never got a definitive answer. A simple tagging program and a few seine nets could have answered a multitude of questions.

The next four days seemed to melt into one long day. It would have been much easier to rent a cabin or check into a motel; the outskirts of Arcadia had dozens of small motels and mom-and-pop restaurants. It would have been nice to get up, eat a stack of pancakes and bacon, and mingle with some of the locals before we slid the canoe in again. We fished a lot, but I can't say we explored much. I have learned over the years that the more time and energy you put into research and preparation, the more interesting the trip. The more time you add for exploration, the better the trip. If you want to enjoy the fishing trip, you need to slow down and remember that fishing is not just about fishing. It's about the people. It's about the culture and the history of the watershed. We need to realize that all we have are each other, the moment, and our memories. Most of all, fishing is about having fun.

Ray suggested that we get off the water early the last day, head southwest, and fish his mysterious lake. It seemed like a great idea, and if I was lucky, we might run into barbecue along the way. We were off the water by ten o'clock and headed south by southwest. We didn't find anything resembling barbecue, but we did run into a few great mom-and-pop breakfast joints. Finally, I found one that looked interesting just outside of North Port Charlotte. We pulled in and had breakfast; the food was good, and the coffee was great.

But Ray was getting a little agitated: he wanted to hit the road and start fishing, whereas I was engaged in conversation with the owner. I was doing my best to explain the proper way to cook and serve pancakes, what the finished product should look like when served. I tried to convince her that the butter should be served at room temperature so it would melt when you slathered it on hot pancakes, not just sit there like an ice cube. I lost her when I said that maple syrup needed to be served warm. The attention to the little things in life makes all the difference.

I would love to tell you where this lake is. It's not hard to find, but it's long since been polluted, and the empty neighborhoods that once surrounded it are now complete. I doubt you would even still have access, and if you did, you wouldn't want to fish it.

When Ray and I first fished it, the lake was pristine. It was full of bass and bluegills and massive bull redfish, and at the right time of the year, baby tarpon. It was a good-sized lake as far as lakes go, and all the canals that lined the empty neighborhoods drained into it. The lake was crystal clear, and at that time, it had white sandy beaches that sloped gently into deeper water. It was unbelievably easy wading. I never found any significant drop-offs. In some ways, it was like wading a sandy flat for bonefish on Deep Water Cay.

We thought about throwing the canoe in and exploring the lake, but that would take too much time, so we decided to wade our way around it. It was midday, and the sun's reflection off the water was almost blinding, even with sunglasses. We didn't make it twenty feet before I hooked my first redfish. My line was melting off the reel way too fast. I thought the big red was going to strip me. However, it didn't seem to want to slow down. I palmed my spool for what it was worth, but it didn't have much effect on the redfish. I had too much line out to make any significant difference. By the time the fish started to slow down, I was down to the last twenty or thirty feet of line. A few seconds later, the fish stopped dead in the water. I took a deep breath and began pumping the fish back. Twenty minutes later, I could see the big redfish struggling on the surface about fifty yards away. It took me another twenty minutes to get the fish close enough so that Ray could pull out the hook and start reviving the brute. I am only guessing, but the fish looked somewhere in the thirty-pound range. It was a monster by any standards.

It had been a long time since I hooked a fish that fast, especially one that big. I was ready to call it a day and head for the barn, but I knew Ray would have a conniption if he knew what I was thinking. We were only twenty feet or so from the Bronco, so I broke down my spinning rod, stuffed it in the back, and strung up my fly rod. I tied on a fluorescent green gurgler I had bought a few weeks earlier at a local hardware store in Sarasota that happens to sell fishing gear.

I miss those days when hardware stores sold fishing gear, outdoor clothing, camping gear, pellet guns, worms, and Dr. Pepper—everything the all-American kid needs. If you were fortunate, they also sold boiled peanuts, the unique southern delight of most good ol' boys. You know the type. They drive around in old pickups with gun racks in the rear window and country music blaring on the radio. Boiled peanuts are right up there with pickled pig's feet and crackers. I can't tell you how much I wanted to catch another big red, but I wanted to get one on a fly this time.

I let Ray take the lead, and I hung back, working my gurgler. I couldn't think of anything better than picking Ray's back pocket. I have no idea who first tied the gurgler, but it looked irresistible, skating and gurgling across the surface. It left behind a trail of bubbles that any fish could stalk. It was so intense. The anticipation was killing me. I was drooling like a rabid dog in the heat and humidity. I would have bet my new Bronco that something had to happen soon. I just knew that it was only a matter of time before another big redfish crushed my fly, the fly rod would arc, the line would scream like a howling banshee, and my soul would turn to stone. I know the mask is a product of mythology and lore, but all myths are based on some truth. I never did get to test the myth: I never sniffed another fish that day.

We must have fished that lake a dozen times over the next several months, and it was always the same. If you worked your butt off, you might get one or maybe two fish per trip. It's hard to believe that the lake had so few fish, but the canals could have had a lot of fish. We almost always saw tarpon rolling on the surface, but they never came close enough to make a decent cast to one. Even when we finally decided to drop the canoe in, the fish always pushed off when we got close. One weekend we decided to paddle up the canals and catch a few bass. The lake didn't have what you might call traditional structure, but the canals were smothered with lily pads and choked with cattails. It looked like a bass fishing paradise.

Rarely did we see other fishermen on the lake, but we occasionally ran into some in the canal system, which begs the question, where did they put in? The canal system wasn't much different from the lake. You had to work hard to catch a few bass. Later that day, I switched to a Shad Rap and tried to dig one out of the deeper water. I was about to give up when a twelve- or thirteen-pound snook followed it to the canoe but never took it. He flashed at the plug and swam away. It was a tough system to crack. In the end, I can only assume that there weren't many fish in the lake or the canals. I've always found that difficult to believe, but the pattern never changed. It was one fish here and there, and then nothing.

The strange part was we never once saw an alligator or any sign of one, or for that matter, any signs of other wildlife, including birds. The lake and the surrounding area seemed devoid of any wildlife. For all practical purposes, the landscape seemed sterile. The last several times Ray and I fished the lake, we found huge skid marks in the grass leading down to the beach, as if a giant gator was sunning itself, and right before we showed up, it slid back into the water. From the girth of its skid marks, the gator had to be eight or nine feet long and maybe two to three hundred pounds. It was definitely big enough to ruin your day.

For the most part, I don't worry too much about alligators, but this was just one gator; because it was a loner, it was probably a male looking for a mate. That meant probably a few females were around there, too. If they happen to be nesting, females can get very territorial. We fished out of the canoe that day and only occasionally got out and waded when we weren't fighting off all the imaginary alligators.

It isn't easy to fish anywhere in South Florida without running into one. This time it was different. Though I never mentioned it to Ray, I was worried it might have been a saltwater crocodile. We were only a few miles from the mouth of the Myakka River. And I knew that at least a few saltwater crocodiles were in the estuary at the mouth of the Myakka River. Florida's saltwater crocodile is relatively docile compared to its African cousin, but it does tend to stick in your craw. It's always the ones you don't see that scare you.

The clock was ticking, my time in Sarasota was winding down, my birthday was right around the corner, the school year was almost over, and I had some serious decisions to make. The last thing I wanted to do was upset the apple cart. Earlier that week, I had told my father I wasn't going to college in the fall, but only after I had received my annual birthday check. He was pissed at me, and why shouldn't he be? He threatened to disown me until I reminded him that he had already done that once, and I didn't think it counted the second time. For the past several years, I had been putting money aside, not much, a few dollars here and there, but enough to get me where I wanted to go.

Most of my surfboards were in various stages of disrepair. Essentially, they were falling apart. We stacked them out in front of the shop and gave most of them away. I kept my two favorite boards, even though I knew they were too short for the surf on the West Coast. They were a big part of my life, and I didn't want to give them up. It's difficult to explain the spiritual side of surfing to someone who's never surfed; it is as important as the adrenalin rush you get from dropping in on a monster wave. It should be intuitive, but for some reason, it's not. After all, we all came from the sea, but very few people still feel that connection.

Ray and I spent the next few days rummaging through all the camping gear my stepfather had given me a few years back. Of course, I couldn't take it all, only the bare necessities. The Bronco was a relatively big truck, but it was deceptive. It didn't hold as much gear as you might think.

At this point, I had been trying to avoid my mother like the plague, but it was time to tell her I was leaving. Who knew when I was coming back? It could be in two or three weeks, or it could be in two or three years. I didn't have any definite plans. The only thing written in stone was that I was headed to the great northwest via Colorado, Wyoming, Montana, Idaho, and eventually to the Oregon coast to chase steelhead. Anything other than that was just a guess.

It was time to spend a few days fishing with Dick and the boys. Next, I called Ralph and Linda to tell them when I was leaving and where I was going. Then I spent time with my sister to say good-bye; Kathy was only seven years old, and I wasn't sure she grasped what I was doing, much less why.

And so it went for the next few weeks.

Finally, late one Friday night at the end of June, I climbed in the Bronco and pointed it north by northwest. Three days later, I was a few hundred miles outside of Denver, headed north along the Continental Divide. It would be years before I saw my friends and family again.

Printed in Great Britain
by Amazon

32043717R00118